College & University Foodservice Management Standards

VOLUME

The L.J. Minor Foodservice Standards Series

College & University Foodservice Management Standards

PETER J. ECKEL, JR.

Food Stores
Michigan State University
East Lansing, Michigan

AVI PUBLISHING COMPANY, INC.
Westport, Connecticut

Cover and frontispiece photographs by Peter J. Eckel, Jr.

Library of Congress Cataloging in Publication Data

Eckel, Peter J.
    College and university foodservice management standards.

    Includes bibliographies and index.
    1. Universities and colleges—Food service.
I. Title.
TX946.E3   1985   647'.95   85-7392
ISBN 0-87055-480-8

ABCDE 4321098765

Printed in the United States of America

This book is dedicated to my family.

To my mother and father and to my aunt and uncle for their love and support during my growing years.

To my wife, who has put up with me for two decades.

To our two children, Peter and Sue, whom we love dearly and wish health, wealth and happiness in the years to come.

Contents

Preface

College and university foodservice has been changing rapidly over the last two decades. Schools have gone from a single-entree menu to four or five selections at each meal, and from one serving—take it or leave it—to a seconds policy that allows students to eat as much as they want. This book considers those standards of good management that are necessary for survival in the increasingly competitive business of college foodservice.

A good foodservice operation can play an important role in attracting students to the school. Chapter 1 discusses how college foodservices can promote productive public relations in order to attract high school students as freshmen and then retain them in the residence halls system as sophomores, juniors and seniors.

Menus—the key to a good foodservice—are discussed in Chapter 2. Chapters 3, 4 and 7 consider the professional purchasing and accounting, expert food handling and careful attention to sanitation that lead to good meals. Chapters 2–4 tell how the interrelated jobs of planning menus, purchasing food and keeping the facilities clean can be done within a limited budget.

Chapter 5 notes that budget considerations must also include food waste, which is especially prevalent in schools that have unlimited food or a seconds policy. The college foodservice operation can play an effective role in convincing students of the importance of food conservation.

As in any business there are the unwanted costs of theft, waste, and carelessness. Chapter 6 emphasizes that a college foodservice must be aware of these "mysterious disappearances" of food, energy and supplies and suggests how to meet the challenge of stopping them.

Chapter 8 explains that the foodservice vending machine operation can be as large or as small as the administration wants. The school must decide whether to be its own vendor or to be contracted to a commercial company. If the vending operation is contracted, it is essential to know the specifics of writing a bid and a contract.

The college foodservice industry demands competence, keeping up with new ideas and trends, and participating in professional societies. One group that is devoted entirely to this segment of the food industry is the National Association of College and University Food Services (NACUFS) (see Chapter 9); other associations have foodservice as part of their organization. A good foodservice operator contributes more to the industry than he or she takes from it. Professionals stay current by subscribing to carefully selected periodicals and by applying the pertinent information, as explained in the Appendix.

This book addresses standards to be followed in running a successful college foodservice. I hope that I have approached many of the topics from a new angle and that the reader can easily implement the ideas and concepts. College foodservice has come a long way in the last decade and good people are needed to continue the momentum with vision enough to meet the management standards of tomorrow.

Acknowledgments

The author would like to express his gratitude to the following friends who helped in making this book possible:

Joe Blair, Oklahoma State University
Jerry Burkhouse, Miami of Ohio
Clark DeHaven, NACUFS
Bud Fontana, University of Virginia
Charlie Gagliano, Michigan State University
Bob Herron, Formerly of Michigan State University
Ed Lappan, Pfeister Corporation
Grace Ordell, University of Virginia
Jim Reath, Central Michigan University
Pat Spaulding, Spaulding Sales, Inc.
Tom Williams, Pfeister Corporation

Special thanks:

Lou Minor, for his interest and unselfish dedication to the advancement of the hotel, restaurant and institutional industry. The sponsorship of this textbook series is just a small sample of that interest.

Ted Smith, who almost got stuck as a co-author, for his ideas and leadership over the years.

Bob Underwood, for his help and friendship.

Doris Ziolkowski and Sandra DeSantis, for their help in typing the drafts from my scribbled writing.

A special, special thanks:

Walter (Jack) Thompson—I could only have taken on the job of writing this book because of his volunteering time at night and on weekends to edit my mistakes.

The L. J. Minor
FOODSERVICE STANDARDS SERIES

Lewis J. Minor, Editor

School of Hotel, Restaurant and
  Institutional Management
Michigan State University
East Lansing, Michigan

1 Public Relations

How would you like to run a commercial business knowing that all of your first-time customers have the preconceived idea that they will dislike you? That is what any college foodservice faces.

Our culture instills in people, from the time they are able to read (or watch), the idea that institutional food is bad. In the comics, Beetle Bailey is served dinner by a fat, slovenly, ash-dropping slob; the dedicated hospital staff on the TV medical show has to eat in a cafeteria where the food is undigestible; the college students in the movie spend half their time avoiding classes, the other half complaining about the dormitory food.

OVERCOMING STUDENTS' PRECONCEPTIONS

The biggest public relations job that any college foodservice has is to show the new student that the meals really are edible. How can foodservice managers do that?

First, they need to serve a good variety of food in a clean, comfortable setting. Second, they must treat their present customers right, for they are the information medium to high school students and new college students—the future customers.

The best public relations ambassadors for college foodservices are adult conferees in the summer. They are able to put the proper money value on what is offered. The question that they ask, time and again, is "You don't serve this to the students, do you?" It is nice to be able to answer "Yes."

A new student arrives at school, eats in a residence hall for the first time—and is pleasantly surprised. The food is not so bad after all! But then a second problem comes creeping into the dining room. Boredom.

Think for a moment of your favorite restaurant. Next, think about eating there, day after day after day—meal after meal after meal—for 1 month, 2 months, 3 months, 4 months. By the end of the second month (maybe even the first), you would start complaining. By the end of the third month, your complaints would become more intense. By the end of the fourth month, your favorite restaurant has probably slipped to the end of your list.

Just think, then, about students in a residence hall who eat in the same place for about nine months of any year. *Boring.* Fortunately, foodservices can do several things to combat the inherent boredom of eating in the same place for weeks on end.

Interesting Meals

It was not too long ago that college foodservices served one entree at each meal. The customers had Hobson's choice—eat it or don't eat it. Today, most schools offer a wide vareity of entrees, as well as many salads, vegetables and desserts. A prime antidote for boring meals is doing something interesting with them. And variety in the menu is just the beginning.

Although it is too difficult and expensive to change the dining room decor every term, there are many small—sometimes unusual—changes that can enliven a foodservice operation. Anything to change the pace. It can be something as simple as using candles and checkered tablecloths for spaghetti night. It can be something as silly as having a Backwards Day with the staff putting their uniforms on backwards, setting the serving lines up in reverse and serving dinner in the morning, lunch at noon and breakfast in the evening.

During an extremely cold and long winter, one cafeteria advertised that dinner Wednesday night was going to be a spring picnic. What they did not say was that all the furniture in the dining room was going to be moved out. Dinner was served on paper plates and the meal consisted of hot dogs, hamburgers, potato salad and potato chips. The inexpensive meal helped compensate for the cost of moving the furniture.

Some schools offer a steak dinner once a week. This could be so often that the novelty and boredom-relieving value are lost. Moreover, in order to serve "steak" that often, a foodservice must use an inexpensive (maybe tenderized) piece of meat or else shift its funds from the rest of the meals that week. An operation only has so much money to spend: If it serves lobster tails and steak on Monday and Tuesday, that leaves only enough money for peanut butter and jelly the other days.

It is probably more effective to offer a good-quality piece of meat and make it

COPYRIGHT ©1982 BY WILLIAM D. CHASE and HELEN M. CHASE

MARCH 31 — THURSDAY

90th Day — Remaining, 275

ANNIVERSARY OF CLAIMED FIRST POWERED FLIGHT. Mar 31. Near Temuka, New Zealand. Richard Pearse, farmer-inventor, flew, according to claim, in monoplane he designed and built, including steerable tricycle undercarriage and internal combustion engine. Pearse flew several hundred yards along a road, landing on a 12-foot-high hedge, on Mar 31, 1903. Pearse commemorative medal was issued on Sept 19, 1971, by Museum of Transport & Technology, Auckland, New Zealand.

BUNSEN BURNER DAY. Mar 31. A day to honor the inventor of the Bunsen Burner, Robert Wilhelm Eberhard von Bunsen, who provided chemists and chemistry students with one of their most indispensable instruments. The Bunsen Burner allowed the user to regulate the proportions of flamable gas and air to create the most efficient flame. Bunsen was born at Gottingen, Germany, on Mar 31, 1811, and was a professor of chemistry at the universities at Kassel, Marburg, Breslau and Heidelberg. He died at Heidelberg, Aug 16, 1899.

DESCARTES, RENE: BIRTHDAY. Mar 31. French philosopher and mathematician, known as the "father of modern philosophy," was born at La Haye, Touraine, France, on Mar 31, 1596. Cartesian philosophical precepts are often remembered because of his famous proposition, "I think, therefore I am," (Cogito ergo sum . . .). Descartes died, of pneumonia, at Stockholm, Sweden, on Feb 11, 1650.

FITZGERALD, EDWARD: BIRTHDAY. Mar 31, 1809. Perhaps best known for his translation of Omar Khayyam's 'Rubaiyat.' Died June 14, 1883.

GOGOL, NIKOLAI VASILEVICH: BIRTHDAY. Mar 31. Russian author of plays novels and short stories, born at Sorochinsk on Mar 31, 1809. He died at Moscow, Mar 4, 1852. Gogol's most famous work was the novel, "Dead Souls."

HAYDN, FRANZ JOSEPH: BIRTHDAY. Mar 31. Franz Joseph Haydn, "father of the symphony," was born at Rohrau, Austria-Hungary, on Mar 31, 1732. He composed about 120 symphonies, more than a hundred works for chamber groups, a dozen operas, and hundreds of other musical works. Haydn died at Vienna, on May 31, 1809.

MALTA: NATIONAL DAY. Mar 31. Republic Day. Festive activities.

MARVELL, ANDREW: BIRTHDAY. Mar 31. English poet born at Winestead, Yorkshire, England, Mar 31, 1621. Died at London, Aug 18, 1678.

MAUNDY THURSDAY. Mar 31. The Thursday before Easter, originally 'dies mandate', celebrates Christ's injunction to love one another, "Mandatus novum do vobis . . ." ("A new commandment I give to you . . .").

MORIONES FESTIVAL. Mar 31-Apr 3. Marinduque Island, Philippine Islands. Province-wide masquarade, Lenten plays and celebrations. (Holy Thursday through Easter Sunday.)

SLEEPING BAG BONSPIEL. Mar 31-Apr 3. Faro, Yukon, Canada. Curling starts Thursday and goes day and night until Sunday afternoon.

VIRGIN ISLANDS: HOLY THURSDAY. Mar 31. Celebrated with evening church services and Holy Communion.

VIRGIN ISLANDS: TRANSFER DAY. Mar 31. Commemorates transfer resulting from purchase of the Virgin Islands by the U.S. from Denmark, Mar 31, 1917, for $25 million.

March	S	M	T	W	T	F	S
1983			1	2	3	4	5
	6	7	8	9	10	11	12
	13	14	15	16	17	18	19
	20	21	22	23	24	25	26
	27	28	29	30	31		

Aprill.

APRIL 1 — FRIDAY

91st Day — Remaining, 274

ALASKA DRYROTTA DAY. Apr 1. Purpose: "To honor the memory of Leinad Moolb, creator of the document now known as 'The Alaska Dryrotta'." Sponsor: Brendan Fog Productions, Attn: Dan Bloom, 883 Basin Rd, Juneau, AK.

APRIL FOOLS' or ALL FOOLS' DAY. Apr 1. "The joke of the day is to deceive persons by sending them upon frivolous and nonsensical errands; to pretend they are wanted when they are not, or, in fact, any way to betray them into some supposed ludicrous situation, so as to enable you to call them 'An April Fool.'" - Brady's Clavis Calendaria, 1812. "The first of April, some do say, Is set apart for All Fools' Day, But why the people call it so, Nor I nor they themselves do know." - Poor Robin's Almanack for 1760.

CANCER CONTROL MONTH. Apr 1-30. Presidential Proclamation. "Always issued for April since 1938." (Pub. Res. No. 82 of Mar 28, 1938). ☆

CANCER CONTROL MONTH. Apr 1-30. In support of the nation's fight against cancer. During this month the American Cancer Society conducts its annual fund raising and educational Cancer Crusade. Sponsor: American Cancer Society, Charles Dahle, Assist VP, Media Relations, 4 W 35th St, New York, NY 10001.

ENGLAND: EASTER FESTIVAL OF SPORT. Apr 1-4. Isle of Man. The festival includes football, rugby, hockey, shooting and athletics. Douglas, Isle of Man.

ENGLAND: SHAKESPEARE THEATRE SEASON. Apr 1. Royal Shakespeare Theatre, Stratford-upon-Avon. Season of plays performed by the world renowned company (April-January). Info from: Box Office, Royal Shakespeare Theatre, Stratford-upon-Avon, Warwickshire, CV37 6BB.

FREEDOM SHRINE MONTH. Apr 1-30. Purpose: To bring America's heritage of freedom to public attention through presentations or rededications of Freedom Shrines by Exchange Clubs. Sponsor: The Natl Exchange Club, Lee Wells, Exec Secy, 3050 Central Ave, Toledo, OH 43606.

GOOD FRIDAY. Apr 1. Observed in commemoration of the crucifixion. Oldest Christian celebration. Possibly corruption of 'God's Friday.' Observed in some manner by most Christian sects everywhere, and as public holiday or part holiday in many places.

INTERNATIONAL FAN CLUB ORGANIZATION FAN ARTIST TOUR. Apr 1-4. London, England. Purpose: To host the IFCO exhibition stand, stage country music showcases and promote fan clubbing and country music on a worldwide basis. Sponsor: Loudilla, Loretta & Kay Johnson, Co-Pres, Box 177, Wild Horse, CO 80862.

INTOLERANCE DAY. Apr 1. Purpose: To limit intolerance to appropriate (All Fools') day. 'Pontificate' today! 'Know all the answers!' Sponsor: The Tolerants, Box 36099, Houston, TX 77236.

FIG. 1.1. Among the many entries in Chases' Calendar, foodservice managers can find numerous ideas for special-event meals.

Menu

Soupe à l'Oignon Gratinée (Onion Soup Gratin)	28%
Crevettes à la Bisque (Shrimp Bisque)	13%
Poulet Grillé Farci au Citron (Lemon Stuffed Baked Chicken)	67%
Sole Gratinée aux Champignons (Sole Gratin with Mushrooms)	11%
Boeuf Bourguignonne (Beef Burgundy)	13%
Clafouti aux Pommes Minceur (French Apple Pancake)	14%
Les Nouvelles Pommes de Terre Rouges (New Red Potatoes)	60%
Asperges (Asparagus)	20%
Chou-Fleur Garni (Steamed Cauliflower with Walnuts)	25%
Salad Nicoise (Salad with Tomatoes)	
Salade de Concombre (Cucumber Salad)	
Pain de Campagne (Croissants)	98%
Mousse au Chocolat (Chocolate Mousse)	67%
Les Tortes (Tortes)	72%
De Fromage et du Fruit (Cheese and Fruit)	
Crêpes Suzette	
Sparkling Catawba	

Salads	*Desserts*
Mixed Greens	Various Cakes and Tortes
Chopped Lettuce	Individual Chocolate Mousse (garnish
Sliced Hard-Cooked Eggs	with whipped cream, almonds or a
Sliced Black Olives	fresh strawberry)
Chopped Green Pepper	20-lb Blocks of Cheese (served with
Anchovies	wood-handled knives)
Green Beans (thawed but uncooked)	Assorted Fresh Fruit—Grapes, Bana-
Tuna	nas, Strawberries, Apples (strewn
Marinated Cucumbers	about the dessert table)
Sliced Red Onions	
Tomatoes	

Sparkling Catawba—poured into disposable champagne glasses into which a
sugar cube soaked in grenadine had been placed

Decorations and Pizzazz

White tablecloths and candles (tapers)
Two-tiered dessert setup/table skirting
Basket of baby's breath and fresh-cut tulips and daffodils on dessert table
Cutouts of French characters, Eiffel Tower, etc., and travel posters
Person in neckkerchief and beret pouring Sparkling Catawba
French records on a stereo for background music
Crêpes Suzette Setup:
　Person making crêpes to-order
　Electric wok
　Small warming pitchers for Grand Marnier
　Crêpes folded in half on glass platter
　Ingredients in small bowl
Decorations—table skirting, white tablecloth, crêpe pan, egg basket (wire),
　fresh eggs, copper whisk
Line Incidentals:
　French flag in serving area
　Special entrée cards written in French
　Soup ready in bowls and garnished with croutons and cheese or paprika
　Extra lemon slices and parsley on the chicken

FIG. 1.2. April in Paris Night.

SUBJECT: Harvest Dinner
DATE AND TIME: Tuesday, October 18   4:00–6:45 p.m.

Menu

Appetizer—Fried Cheese (Swiss and Cheddar),
    Chilled Apple Cider

Breaded Pork Chops	36%
Turkey Breast, sliced	67%
Fried Perch	16%
Cheddar Vegetable Sandwich	5%
Hamburger	12%

Baked Potatoes
Corn Bread Dressing
Squash Halves, fresh
Asparagus
Rice with Chicken Gravy

From Central Bakery:
    Spice Layer Cake
    Cheese Cake, Plain and Strawberry
    Peach Cobbler
    Pumpkin Bread
    Dinner Rolls

Decorations

Six-foot table with white tablecloths and white drapes on entering staircase landing for appetizer. Baskets with fruit, Indian corn, and fall leaves were used as centerpiece. Draped dessert serving table in center of dining room composed of four six-foot rectangular tables. Centerpiece composed of fall leaves, horn of plenty filled with fruit and gourds.

Comments: Have several extra student employees help prepare desserts, decorate and serve cider and cheese. Use chafing dishes to keep fried cheese hot.

FIG. 1.3.   Harvest Dinner.

a real special occasion at midterms or maybe finals. During the fall term, steak night may be unnecessary as the newness of school, football season and Thanksgiving help alleviate students' boredom with the foodservice.

The best time for fancy meals is winter and spring. Winter, especially at northern schools, can be a very boring season, and spring is a time for trying to recruit students for the next year.

Antipasto Trays—these trays take a good deal of time to make up but went over very well. We started the meal with six complete trays and had to refill them all once. The Italian bread sticks, which were obtained through food stores on a special order, were also very popular. We had two setups in the dining room, and there was little crowding around the trays because of this.

Minestrone Soup—We made 7 gallons of soup and had very little left over with our 827 count.

Neapolitan Pork Parmesan—This was our only "firsts" item and it ran 36%. We made 300 servings and had only 2 servings left when the line closed.

Italian Slivered Beef on a Bun—Unsure of the demand for this sandwich, we cooked and slivered 225 lb of beef but marinated only about 75% of it. It was our most popular entree for this dinner at 72%, but we did not need to marinate over 150 lb of beef.

Fettuccine Alfredo—The fettuccine ran 18% and was really a very good item. Although not very high in percentage, we had a lot of good comments from the people who did try it.

Sole Florentine Amandine—This was our one "surprise" item. We thought we were well prepared with close to 100 servings, but it ran over 16% and we had to quickly prepare another 10 lb of fish.

Pastas and Marinara Sauce—Instead of running a potato dish, we decided to offer different pasta shapes with a red sauce as a side dish. We ran close to 70 lb of seashell macaroni and mostaccioli noodles. Because we wanted this to be a side dish, we gave out smaller portions than we would on spaghetti night unless it was requested as a main entree.

Fried Eggplant—We planned on using 2 cases of eggplant, but the item was so popular that we ran out about three quarters of the way through the meal.

Italian Green Beans with Tomatoes—We planned to use 2 cases of green beans for this vegetable but used 1½ cases instead.

The Central Bakery was very helpful in making our dinner a success. They provided us with all the special breads, cakes and cookies. The Zucchini Bread and Rum Torte were especially good.

Comments: There were about 5 hours of extra labor needed the day before this dinner to get the beef slivered and marinated and to get the items ready to assemble on the antipasta trays. There was an additional 5 hours of labor needed the day of the dinner to assemble the trays and do some additional prep. After the meal got underway it was a very easy meal to run as we ran out of very few items. The Shaw Hall Advisory Staff did a super job of serving desserts and coffee and helped make this dinner well liked and accepted by the students.

FIG. 1.4.   Italian Dinner—actual report.

Special Events

Every day in the year is designated as a special day of some sort. *Chases' Calendar of Annual Events*, published by Contemporary Books, Inc. (180 North Michigan Avenue, Chicago, IL 60601) lists these days. Some are as common as Valentine's Day, Thanksgiving and Christmas, others as unknown as Casey Jones' birthday, Be-Late-for-Something-Day and Boxing Day. This book is well worth the price (about $15) to get some monotony-breaking ideas. Figure 1.1 is a sample page of Chases' Calendar.

A list of some other types of monotony breakers follows:

Banana split night	Burger bar
Birthday night (for the school,	Cheese night
hall, football coach, etc.)	Dessert night

Menu

Eggs in a Cloud	20%
Scrambled Eggs	50%
Eggs Sunnyside	20%
Eggs Over Easy	20%
Eggs, Hardboiled	2%
Eggs, Softboiled, to order	
French Toast/Powdered Sugar	20%
Blueberry Pancakes	20%
Smokies	30%
Bacon	30%
Hashbrowns au Gratin	90%
Glazed Cinnamon Rolls	
Biscuits/Honey	

Decorations and Line Garnish

Red and white checked tablecloths, hurricane candles optional. Order enough extra tablecloths for use the entire day. Wicker cornucopia with available fruits and vegetables placed on serving line.

Eggs in a Cloud Preparation

In vegetable dish, place English muffin half, then cooked sausage pattie, then beaten egg white. Place poached egg in center of egg white, put in oven to set egg white (1 min.), garnish with parsley.

FIG. 1.5. Lumberjack Breakfast Buffet.

Ethnic dinners: Hot fudge special
    Black   Oriental   Movie night
    Canadian   Polish   Nacho bar
    Italian   Swedish   Strawberry shortcake night
    Mexican   Tater buffet night

Do not forget specials or monotony breakers for breakfast and lunch: lumber-jack breakfast, pancake day (serve two varieties of them at all three meals), soup and sandwich lunch, soup day, apple day, cherry day. Six actual menu ideas and

---

Menu

Cream of Mushroom Soup	20%
Carved Rounds of Beef	80%
Fried Cod	11%
Ratatouille Omelets	15%
Italian Sausage/Spartan Rolls	20%
Mashed Potatoes Supreme	

Cauliflower   Fruit Cocktail
Green Beans   German Chocolate Cake
                        Soft Serve

Popcorn

Borrow popcorn machine from the grill.
Buy most of the popcorn prepopped.
1 extra person for the popcorn machine.

Setup

2 screens, 2 stands, 2 16-mm projectors from IMC.
Set up on each side of the cafeteria.
Had 6 films.
Films average 10 minutes each.
Must order films 7 days in advance from Lansing Public Library or 14 days in
    advance from East Lansing Public Library. (Limit 3 per person)
Screen, projector and operator must be booked 3 days in advance with IMC.
Cost: Projectors $15.00 each; screens $12.00 each.

Conclusion

This event was run without changing the menu (except adding the popcorn).
The residents loved the idea.

FIG. 1.6. Movie Night.

Menu

Egg Drop Soup	48%
Egg Rolls/Plum & Mustard Sauce	100%
Terriyaki Beef	34%
Sweet & Sour Chicken	34%
Shrimp Subgum	34%
Meatless Egg Foo Young	8%
Hamburgers	28%
Stir fry vegetables	49%
Fried rice	150%*
Steamed rice	90%

Beef Gravy for Egg Foo Young
Dinner Rolls
Fortune Cookies
Almond Cookies
Orange Sherbet
Fresh Fruit Cup (Apples, Bananas, Pine-
apple, Oranges, Pears, Watermelon)

*150% due to use with the entree and as a
side dish.

Pan and Line Garnishes

Line: Pineapple halves with Bird of Paradise on them
Pan: Terriyaki Beef—Tomato Roses
Sweet and Sour Chicken—Chunks of pineapple, tomato wedges, and
green peppers sprinkled over it
Hamburgers—Umbrellas
Egg Foo Young—Carrot flowers
Cookies—One of each kind on a plate
Sherbet—Mint leaf
Very simple garnishes but very colorful.

Decorations

Wall hangings
Oriental fans & lights
Table with oriental artwork & trinkets
Kites with long tails
A giant fish kite with a fan blowing on it to make it swim
Kimonos—2 students drssed in them to serve the soup. (A person from the
International Center came over to tie them properly.)

FIG. 1.7. Oriental Dinner.

write ups from different foodservices are shown in Figs. 1.2–1.7. The percentages refer to the number of people selecting a particular item.

Involving a student food committee, hall council, etc., in the planning of special dinners can be helpful in arousing student interest; it also can be very educational to the students by acquainting them with the costs of a foodservice operation.

Montony breakers have a tendency to match the personality of the foodservice manager or director. They can be as different and crazy as the person is. Managers who have great rapport with the students can get away with almost anything.

MEETING THE COMPETITION

Up until the early 1980s most people did not think of colleges and universities as being in competition with anyone. Students were plentiful and many schools were spending their efforts on constructing new buildings. Even then schools were in competition with each other, they just did not pay a lot of attention to it. But with fewer and fewer students graduating from high schools, colleges and universities now rely on public relations and recruiting to attract new students.

I am not naive enough to think that a student chooses a particular university just because he or she knows it has a good foodservice. On the other hand, I am sure that some choose one school over another because it offers a good program in their academic field *and* has a good foodservice. The foodservice can add to, or detract from, the overall appeal of a school to a prospective student.

Competition in our business does not stop with high school seniors but continues throughout their undergraduate and graduate years. During these years, colleges compete with off-campus foodservices and apartments.

If a school does not meet the needs of its customers, they will go to other schools and off-campus businesses that do. Meeting customer needs is not enough. Public relations is necessary to let faculty, staff, students, parents and the rest of the world know that a college's foodservice gives good value for the dollar.

One way to evaluate the competitive position of a restaurant is in terms of the four main features of its operation: food, decor, service and price. A popular marketing concept states that when pricing is competitive (that is, similar among restaurants), customers will flock to those establishments that furnish excellence in two out of the remaining three features.

For example, a restaurant that has excellent food and excellent service with average decor is in a good competitive position. One with excellent service and excellent decor along with average food, also is likely to have a steady line of customers. Similarly, an establishment with excellent food and excellent decor coupled with average service will survive in hard times.

Although this marketing concept is designed for fancy restaurants or clubs, either on or off campus, I think it has some application to all foodservices. It can provide a rough indication of the competitive position of a college foodservice in relation to off-campus restaurants and the foodservices at other schools.

ASSESSING STUDENT OPINIONS

One of the most direct ways to assess the operation of a foodservice is to find out what its customers think about it, and what, if anything, they would like changed. This can be done using several different techniques: informal survey, written questionnaires, dish room test, or suggestion box. Be warned, however, that students may complain that "the food is bad," but when asked for specifics, offer only vague generalizations.

Informal Surveys

Simple ways of taking an informal student survey include table hopping or standing at the dining room entrance or exit and asking customers their opinions. Though easy and relatively inexpensive to conduct, informal surveys of this type have some disadvantages.

First, only a few, quite simple questions can be asked. Second, responses to this type of survey are likely to be spontaneous and not very well thought out. In general, such responses will reflect customers' most recent experiences with a foodservice. When asked, "Is the soup hot?" they have a tendency to remember only the last one or two times they ate.

Questionnaires

A more formal survey method involves the use of written questionnaires. Students can be asked either to fill these out right then or to take them back to their rooms and return them completed the next day. The latter approach is likely to produce more complete and thought-out responses that give a better overall impression of student opinion about a foodservice. However, many of the students given a questionnaire to take with them will not fill out and return it, so the number of responses is likely to be less than with surveys conducted on the spot.

During the last few years, the foodservice at Michigan State University has distributed questionnaires in students' mailboxes. By asking the same questions each year, this foodservice has obtained a year-to-year progress report—is it doing better, worse or the same as previous years?

Because most students have been ingrained with the marks of A, B, C, D and F used on their report cards, it is a good idea to use these same response categories in a questionnaire. For example, students can be instructed to respond to each question with one of the five "marks," defined as follows:

A—Outstanding
B—Better than average
C—Average
D—Below average
F—Failure

A typical foodservice should strive for marks of average or above (i.e., A, B or C); a high percentage of D or F responses would indicate problem areas. A fancy restaurant on campus should expect A and B responses; C, D and F responses would suggest the need for considerable improvement in a high-class operation.

Michigan State uses the questionnaire shown in Table 1.1. The percentages are the responses received in the top three categories (A, B and C) during 2 years.

Dish Room Test

All the surveys in the world cannot compare in speed and accuracy to the dish room test, commonly used in all phases of the food business. A dish room test entails nothing more than watching the dishes being returned to the dish room. If a product is bad, there will be a lot of it going into the garbage. Of course, discovering *why* a particular food is unacceptable to many customers may take some detective work.

Suggestion Boxes

Sometimes I wish all restaurants had suggestion boxes and forms to fill out so that I could tell management what a poor meal, service or sanitation program it has.

I will often tell a waitress or cashier what I think is wrong with a restaurant, but I wonder how many times my comments get passed on to someone who can do something about the problem. If I leave my opinions in writing in a suggestion box, at least they should be read by someone in authority.

There are many different ways to set up a suggestion box system. I know of one manager who had two boxes side by side: one was for suggestions and one for demands. Needless to say most of the forms were placed in the demand box. Figure 1.8 is a complaint form that asks for suggestions and, notice, compliments as well.

Sometimes complaints are actually backhanded compliments. For example, a foodservice customer might ask, "Why do you serve both Monte Cristo sand-

TABLE 1.1. Foodservice Questionnaire Used at Michigan State University

	Percentage of responses in A, B and C categories	
Questions and response categories	1st year	2nd year

For questions 1–8 mark one of the following responses:
  A. Very satisfied
  B. Somewhat satisfied
  C. Neutral
  D. Somewhat dissatisfied
  F. Very dissatisfied

	1st year	2nd year
1. Are you satisfied with the variety of entrees served?	65.0	66.4
2. Of the entrees you like, do you consider them well prepared?	69.1	72.7
3. Are you satisfied with the variety of vegetables served?	66.2	63.6
4. Do you consider them well prepared?	52.6	56.2
5. Are you satisfied with the variety of desserts served?	84.5	84.5
6. Do you consider them well prepared?	85.0	85.2
7. Are you satisfied with the variety of salads served?	74.0	82.9
8. Do you consider them well prepared?	77.3	85.6

9. Is the cafeteria a pleasant place for you to eat? 91.9 94.3
  A. Very pleasant
  B. Somewhat pleasant
  C. Neutral
  D. Somewhat unpleasant
  F. Very unpleasant
10. Are the silverware, china, and glasses clean? 83.5 83.7
  A. Always
  B. Almost always
  C. Usually
  D. Quite often not
  F. Never
11. Are the tables, carpet, and serving area clean? 91.4 92.2
  A. Always
  B. Almost always
  C. Usually
  D. Quite often not
  F. Never
12. Do you like the way the foods are displayed? 85.2 88.8
  A. Like very much
  B. Generally like
  C. Neutral
  D. Dislike somewhat
  F. Dislike very much
13. Do you feel your hall's foodservice offers enough special events, such as ethnic theme dinners, cheese nights, etc.? 66.1 66.1
  A. Just the right number
  B. Not quite as many as I would like
  C. Neutral
  D. Not nearly enough
  F. Don't care

(continued)

TABLE 1.1. *(Continued)*

Questions and response categories	Percentage of responses in A, B and C categories	
	1st year	2nd year
14. How would you evaluate the planning and carrying out of these special events? Leave blank if you have no opinion. A. Excellent B. Good C. Fair D. Needs improvement F. Poor	83.3	82.6
15. Do you feel the foodservice staff is interested in pleasing you? A. They try very hard to please me. B. They have a strong interest in my needs. C. They usually show some interest in my needs. D. They show a slight concern. F. They don't care at all.	73.6	71.2
16. Generally, are you satisfied with the foodservice in your cafeteria? A. It satisfies all my needs. B. It satisfies most of my needs. C. It does an adequate job. D. It is less than satisfactory. F. It falls way short.	75.4	78.2
17. Is your *hot* food served hot? A. Always B. Most of the time C. About half the time D. Usually not F. Seldom	73.4	70.5
18. Is your *cold* food served cold? A. Always B. Most of the time C. About half the time D. Usually not F. Seldom	93.7	93.5
19. Do you feel that the management is responsive to reasonable requests? A. Always B. Usually C. Sometimes D. Usually not F. Never	89.3	88.2
20. Some of the more costly entrees are not available for seconds. Do you feel this is a reasonable policy? A. Very reasonable B. Somewhat reasonable C. Neutral or undecided D. Somewhat unreasonable F. Very unreasonable	75.7	74.8

TABLE 1.1. (*Continued*)

Questions and response categories	Percentage of responses in A, B and C categories	
	1st year	2nd year
21. When you want a second serving, is there a "seconds" item available that satisfies you? A. Always B. Usually C. About half the time D. Seldom F. Never	81.4	82.1
22. How do you feel about the frequency with which sandwiches are served at dinner? A. Way too often B. Somewhat too often C. Just often enough D. Not quite often enough F. Not nearly enough	75.9	76.5
23. Generally, a breakfast item (pancakes, waffles, eggs, etc.) is offered at Saturday lunch. What is your reaction? A. Enjoy very much B. Enjoy occasionally C. Don't care either way D. Would prefer a regular lunch item F. Dislike	76.7	84.9
24. Do you prefer that a breakfast item be offered at Sunday dinner? A. Always B. Usually C. Occasionally D. Seldom F. Never	56.3	59.2

	Percentages of the two highest categories selected	
25. How often would you like hamburgers made available? Select the answer that most closely matches your preference. A. Every lunch, every other dinner B. Every lunch only C. Every other lunch, every other dinner D. Every other lunch only F. Less frequently than the above	28.6 62.1	24.0 60.3
26. How often would you like hot dogs made available? Select the answer that most closely matches your preference. A. Every lunch, every other dinner B. Every lunch only C. Every other lunch, every other dinner D. Every other lunch only F. Less frequently than the above	14.8 40.6	16.0 47.8

WE VALUE YOUR IDEAS!
We want to please you and can do a better job if we have your help. Please share your ideas, suggestions and comments

If we're not doing something right, let us know. We'll try to improve.

Just drop your suggestion in the box. Be specific so that we can take positive action.

Oh yes, we're glad to get compliments too. We share them with out staff—makes them feel good!

My comments about the residence halls are _____

_____

_____

_____

_____

_____

If you want a direct reply: Name _____

Date _____   Room Number _____

                               Phone Number _____

FIG. 1.8.   Sample form for soliciting student complaints, and compliments, about a college foodservice.

wiches and Burritos at the same meal? I can't eat both.'' Sure it is a complaint, but at the same time the student is saying, "Hey, I like both of those items, let's split them up to different days."

Suggestions run from being obscene and dumb, all the way to being helpful for managers trying to improve their operation. If nothing else, suggestion boxes act as an outlet for students' frustrations. Sometimes the frustration has nothing to do with the foodservice operation. It might be academic, home life, love life or even a losing football season.

The secret to a good suggestion box system is to let customers know that someone in authority is listening to what they say. As a foodservice manager, you may not be able to do what students suggest, or correct the problems they complain about. Still, it is helpful to get back to them and explain your position. If students understand why something about the foodservice is the way it is, or why you cannot do certain things, they may not like the situation, but they will probably dislike it less. It is important, then, to follow up on suggestions by contacting the students who submit them. This can be as simple as talking to the students the next time you see them in the dining room; or you might go to their room and discuss their concerns on their turf.

Some people thrive on being known and recognized—even if it is only by "the old foodservice manager." As you see Peter or Sue in the dining room, ask them how things are going. If they had complained about the soup being cold, ask how the soup has been the last few days. In some cases the soup may not have changed one degree in temperature, but the students' reaction has: "It's just great—thanks for getting the cooks to keep it hotter."

Contacting suggestion makers by telephone leaves something to be desired, but you made the effort to call. The problem is that a phone call is very impersonal, just a voice in the passing night. The students will see you in the dining room and know they talked to you, but will you know who they are?

A very effective method of responding to suggestions and complaints is to visit with students in their rooms to discuss the problem. You may think that certain complaints—for example, that the soup is cold or that the orange juice tastes weak—are too unimportant to justify your taking the time. But almost any suggestion or complaint can lead into a long discussion on finances, union restrictions, etc.—factors affecting your decisions that students rarely think about. This gives you an excellent opportunity to educate students about how your foodservice operates. Such informal, indirect public relations is often more effective than some expensive publicity campaign.

INVOLVING PARENTS

Public relations and communication with parents are very important for college and university foodservices. True, the immediate customers are the students, but often Mom and Dad are footing the bill. And most parents have a genuine interest in all aspects of the children's college life.

During the last year of high school, they had shared an excitement with their student of receiving mail from different colleges, talking about college life and getting them ready to leave the nest. There was a flurry of activity in August as the student was getting ready to leave. Now, the day comes and all head for school in a mad rush.

For the student this madness continues with registration, new friends, football games, parties, etc. Poor old Mom and Dad drive home—and, for them, everything stops.

The house is quiet; meal preparations are cut down. There is one less person to yell at, pick up after and talk to. The sharing of the child's life stops. Who are they dating, what is going on in classes, are they eating properly, getting enough sleep? All of this information comes to a halt. Even the mail from the school stops.

The only contact they have is a periodic telephone call and an occasional letter (usually asking for money). The school's foodservice can fill the void by offering a variety of products, e.g., cakes, cookies, candy, pizza, etc., and create good will between the school and the forgotten Mom and Dad at home.

Final Exam Kits

Every school is faced with the profit seeker who mails a flyer to parents, advertising a Finals Week Kit. It goes something like this:

Dear Parents:
    Your student is entering a time where a special thought from home will be a big morale booster. Final exams are coming up, your student will be studying hard and long into the night to establish or to maintain grades. How about a FINALS SURVIVAL KIT to keep your student going?
    Send me a check for $9.75, and the day before finals start, a kit containing cookies, fresh fruit, candy and a gift will be delivered to your student.
    Your student misses you and home. A simple thought from home at this time is worth any price. Just make out a check for $9.75 and send it to FINALS SURVIVAL KIT COMPANY, P.O. Box 99, and make your child happy.

All the ingenious people who start this type of fly-by-night operation have their own way of selling the program. Usually the kit consists of goods worth about $1.50 to $2.00. The "gift" is a five-cent balloon or maybe a plastic ring worth about the same. The cookies are left over from World War I, and the fruit is a plum, a banana or a prune or two.

Unfortunately, a number of parents will respond to this come-on. Then they find out the kit was worth only a couple of dollars, or maybe was not even delivered. The college is a number of miles away and P.O. Box 99 has been reassigned to someone else. So they blame the school, if for no other reason than just for allowing this activity to go on. There is nothing the school can do, but they receive the negative comments.

A school could take this idea (it is a good one) and turn it into a legitimate service for students and parents—and a public relations tool for the college. The registrar or housing office can provide a computer printout of addresses for direct mailings.

A simple way to administer such offers is to sell coupons to parents that students can turn in for various products—e.g., hamburgers and soft drinks in cash outlets. If a foodservice has an ice cream parlor, pizza operation or beer rathskeller, special coupons can be offered to parents as a finals week offering from home. Or how about a package for two, either for a date or roommate: two subs and a liter of soft drink, beer, wine, a sundae at the ice cream parlor. One price for a regular sundae, another for a sundae for two and a third for a wheelbarrow sundae for 30. Coupons for candy is another possibility.

Michigan State University has implemented two direct mail offers to parents: a finals week cookie survival kit and birthday cakes. The operation of these services is described in the next two sections.

Cookies from Home

Three weeks before final exams, a mailing is sent to the parents of students living in residence halls (Fig. 1.9). Four packages are offered at different prices. Figure 1.10 is the return envelope/order form that is enclosed. As a cost savings, Michigan State University uses the same envelope for both its final exam kit and birthday cake offers. This also gives cross-advertising for the two.

The most successful end of term has been in the fall, followed by winter, with the end of spring term turning out to be a money loser. The average return percentages over several years illustrate this: fall, 12%; winter, 8%; and spring, 4%.

Michigan State did not start this project as a money maker but as a public relations tool with both parents and students. However, the cookie packages will cover all costs when the return rate is a little more than 4% (Table 1.2). If the return rate is higher than this breakeven level, some income is generated for debt retirement—a welcome by-product of the service.

A computer printout on gum labels of the students' home addresses is used for the mailing. The bulk mail rate reduces costs. After the parents' check is received, the orders are compiled and the cookies are baked in the university's central bake shop the night before delivery. If a school does not have the facilities to bake fresh cookies, an arrangement may be made with a local baker to provide them.

Each of the residence halls at Michigan State has a reception desk to act as an information center and take care of mail distribution. A note is placed in a recipient's mailbox informing him or her that a package is being held. Upon proper identification, the student signs for the cookies—then enjoys them.

A variation of this service—"Cookie of the Month Club"—has been considered but not implemented at Michigan State. In this service, a cookie box would be delivered once each month to a student's residence hall. Order forms would be distributed to parents during summer orientation and fall check-in; they also could be mailed during registration week in the fall term, scheduled to arrive just as parents are starting to miss their children.

Payment by parents would be in advance, at the time of sign-up. This would allow the school to invest the money, but would force parents to come up with a big cash outlay in the fall. This could be hard for many families to do and might reduce participation.

Another potential problem would be the difficulty of keeping track of where

send cookies

As the school work stacks up,
   with mid-terms and finals ready to pile the books even higher,
your student at MSU needs sympathy, affection,
   and cookies

If you will supply the first two, we will take care of the cookies.

When you return the enclosed order form,
   within 72 hours after we receive it
we will deliver a box of fresh cookies, with a message from you,
   right to the student's residence hall.

If you prefer a cake, we are pretty good at that too.

And how about for some other special occasion —
   birthday, graduation —
you name it, we will deliver.

—The On-Campus Bakers
230 Brody Hall
Michigan State University
East Lansing, Michigan 48824

FIG. 1.9.   Mailing sent to parents by Michigan State University foodservice offering "cookies from home" and birthday cake service.

PLEASE DELIVER:

| DECORATED CAKES | ■■ Chocolate Icing ☐ Choclate Cake | ☐ White Icing ☐ Chocolate Cake | ▨ Chocolate Icing ☐ Yellow Cake | ☐ White Icing ☐ Yellow Cake |

Size Cake   9″x13″ ($9.00) ☐   13″x17″ ($15.50) ☐

JUMBO COOKIES (4″)

Oatmeal _____ doz.   Peanut Butter ___ doz.

Chocolate Chip ___ doz.   Combination ___ doz. (some of all 3 kinds)

Total Dozens Cookies

_____ at $3.50/doz. = $ _____

DATE TO BE DELIVERED

TO: Student's name _____

Address _____ Total enclosed $ _____

(We are unable to deliver off-campus, to sororities, fraternities, off-campus apartments, etc.)

Make check payable to Michigan State University

If you write a message on the enclosed gift card, we will deliver it with the cookies; or use it to tell us what to write on the cake.

Cakes and Cookies ARE
Delivered Monday – Friday ONLY

☆

FOR SPECIAL OCCASIONS, SUCH AS BIRTHDAYS, OR DURING EXAM PERIOD, MICHIGAN STATE UNIVERSITY'S ON-CAMPUS BAKE SHOP WILL DELIVER A DECORATED CAKE OR A BOX OF JUMBO COOKIES TO STUDENTS LIVING ON-CAMPUS.

Orders should be made at least 2 weeks in advance, using this envelope.

☆

FIG. 1.10. Return envelope–order form used at Michigan State University for "cookies from home" and birthday cake mailings.

students are living. Michigan State University has 15,000 room changes a year (an average of about one per student per year). The record keeping necessary to locate students each month could make the costs of such a program prohibitive.

Birthday Cakes

Michigan State's birthday cake service is handled in the same general way as the "cookies from home." A computer printout is sent to the central bakery each month listing the names, home addresses and dates of birth for students with birthdays the succeeding month. A mailing (Fig. 1.11) is sent to the parents (again, using the bulk rate).

TABLE 1.2.   Cookie Sales Report for Spring Term

Number of mailings sent: 15,229
Number of orders received: 644,   4.2%

Revenues Item	Quantity	Cost/doz ($)	Total income ($)
Oatmeal jumbos	68	3.50	238.00
Peanut butter jumbos	83.5	3.50	292.25
Chocolate chip jumbos	386.5	3.50	1352.75
Combination jumbos	552.5	3.50	1933.75
Total revenues	1090.5		3816.75

Expenditures	Cost	Percentage of income
Order form and envelope	1522.90	39.9
Postage	456.87	12.0
Labor (stuffing, packaging, delivery)	540.00	14.2
Food cost	1053.86	27.6
Packing box	235.29	6.2
Total expenditures	3808.92	99.9
Net available for debt retirement	7.83	0.2[a]

Average order $3816.75 ÷ 644 = $5.93/order (1.7 doz/order)

[a]Discrepancy due to round-off error.

The response to the birthday cake offer has been impressive—much higher than is typical for the usual direct mail offering. Over the years, the response rate has been in the range of 20–22%, based on the number of students whose birthdays occur when the university is in session. Table 1.3, a financial report on birthday cake sales, shows that two types of cake are offered. A birthday cake service has the potential of generating substantial revenues for a foodservice.

TABLE 1.3.   Birthday Cake Sales Report for the School Year

Number of mailings sent: 6794
Number of orders received: 1505,   22.1%

Revenues Item	Quantity	Cost	Total income ($)
Cake Style A	1015	$9.00	$9,135
Cake Style B	490	15.50	7,595
Total revenues	1505		$16,730

Expenditures	Cost ($)	Percentage of income
Card and return envelope	518	3
Postage	251	2
Decorating labor and delivery	4551	27
Food cost	2744	16
Packaging	686	4
Total expenditures	$8750	52
Money available for debt retirement	$7980	48

Would you like to give
a special birthday cake
to your student at
    Michigan State University?

MSU's own
    on-campus bake shop
    will deliver
    a decorated cake
    right to the residence hall.

It doesn't have to be
    for a birthday, however.
We will decorate a cake
    for any occasion.

And it doesn't have
    to be a cake.
We will also deliver
    fresh cookies
    right to the hall.

Why not surprise your student.
    The enclosed order form
    will tell you how.

— The On-Campus Bakers
at MSU

FIG. 1.11. Mailing sent to parents of MSU students to promote birthday cake service. Note cross-advertising between the mailings for cookies and cakes.

PERPETUATING THE BAD FOOD MYTH

While schools are spending time and money promoting the positive aspects of their foodservice, many students are instituting their own public relations campaign.

Earlier in this chapter, I mentioned the problem of the preconceptions high school seniors have about college foodservices. Without ever having eaten in a residence hall, they know the food is not very good. This same concept is also planted in the minds of parents. Yet contrary to expectations, foodservice at most schools turns out to be very acceptable. After 2–3 weeks at school, students discover the food is not so bad. In fact, some students have never eaten so well. Why then does the bad food myth persist?

One reason is that some students see a chance to con Mom and Dad. If parents already believe the food is bad—starchy, greasy, unpalatable—why not play it for all it is worth. During a student's freshman year, this con game might pay off in money for movies, maybe a new sweater or pair of shoes, or better yet, a weekend trip to the beach or mountains. Parents, sitting at home, have only their child's long-suffering complaints to go by. Parental sympathies, and pocketbooks, are likely to be extended.

There is more to this negative food business than just pocket money. Later in college, those students wanting to move off campus to an apartment must convince their parents that it is to the advantage of the entire family.

Watch out; here comes the bad food routine again. For good measure throw in how noisy it is in the halls. "Can't study, can't eat, can't sleep, can't do anything in the hall." The student's saving grace is to move into an apartment. "And by the way, Dad, it is so much cheaper to live off campus."

The blame for perpetuating the bad food myth does not rest solely on students; it may come in handy for parents. too. Mom and Dad are very proud of the fact that their child is smart enough to be accepted to college. If their student flunks out, parents do not want to admit that their son or daughter was too dumb to make it, so the excuses start. The food was bad, everyone knows that. It was too noisy, and who can study with all that racket? In a large school, the classes are too big; and in a small school, the facilities are inadequate. The school is cutting expenses and graduate assistants were teaching the courses. All of this to protect family ego.

In time, Aunt Marion and Uncle Bob tell their friends why their niece or nephew flunked out. It just happens that their friends have a high school student that is getting ready to go to college. Now *that* family is preconditioned to expect bad food. Here we go again!

COMMUNICATING WITH STUDENTS

Student Employees

Student employees can help a foodservice maintain communications with other students. If encouraged to do so, student workers can keep management informed of the concerns their friends have about a foodservice. If the relationship with student employees is developed properly, it becomes not "your" foodservice but "our" foodservice.

Suggestions can be solicited from student workers on an informal one-on-one basis or at more formal meetings held periodically. Even if the foodservice management cannot do what they want (probably because of finances), it has an interested—and to some degree, captive—audience as to why something cannot be done. These students, in turn, will serve as a common link to other students, passing on information about foodservice policies and operations.

In most cases the information is diluted, but the general idea gets through. This, in turn, can stimulate other students to ask for further clarification about specific conerns. There are many, far-reaching benefits for a foodservice manager in having student employees that are satisfied in their jobs.

Student Customers

Getting to know student customers should be an important objective of any foodservice manager. People thrive on knowing someone in charge, knowing what is going on, feeling they have an influence on the operation.

New supervisors or cafeteria managers sometimes tend to avoid the hectic periods by doing office work. If an operation serves only during certain periods and is closed during others, all supervisors should be in the kitchen, on the serving line, or in the dining room during meal hours. The foodservice manager is, after all, in charge. If the foodservice manager is in the office, in reality that function automatically switches to someone else.

An operation that runs all day will have its busy and slow periods. Managers should be in the serving and dining areas during peak sales. They can do their office work, and take meals and breaks during slow periods.

I might point out that slow periods are the worst time for customers to eat in any restaurant or cafeteria. About a half hour to an hour after the rush period, the service and food takes a dive. This is the period where everyone from the cook to the server to the waitress slows down. The food is cold, overcooked or slow in getting out of the kitchen. The waitress is taking a break or preparing for the next meal. The server is cleaning up or going to the bathroom. The supervisor is doing paperwork in the office or has gone to a meeting.

The most neglected part of any operation is the time just after the peak until the closing of that meal period. However, the customer that comes in 2 minutes before closing should have the same food served in the same friendly manner as the customer that comes in just before the peak.

That is a tough goal, but foodservice managers, who want to establish good public relations with their clientele, set that as one of their primary objectives.

School Newspapers

In the past, especially when colleges only offered one entree per meal, the letters to the editor section of the student newspaper frequently had complaints about the foodservice. With improved menus and a more determined effort by schools for quality and customer satisfaction, these complaints have subsided. A student newspaper can be a very useful means of communicating with students. At a number of schools, the newspaper prints informational articles about the foodservice and its staff. Some schools even have a dining hall staff member as a contributing writer. Such articles might be primarily educational, focusing on some aspect of nutrition of particular relevance to college students. At other times. they might be partly promotional, focusing on special events or new services planned by the foodservice.

Whatever the arrangement at a particular school, the student newspaper—as well as student magazines and newsletters—can be valuable public relations tools for the foodservice. Just remember that effective public relations, regardless of the form it takes, depends on the honest, persuasive communication of information relevant to the needs and interests of the audience.

REFERENCES

BLOMSTROM, R. L. Strategic Marketing Planning in the Hospitality Industry. Educational Institute of the American Hotel and Motel Association, East Lansing, MI.

FAIRBROOK, P. 1979. College and University Food Service Manual. Colman Publishers, Stockton, CA.

GUTHRIE, H. A. 1978. Is education not enough? J. Nutr. Ed. *10*, 57.

PIZAM, A., LEWIS, R. C., and MANNING, P. B. 1982. The Practice of Hospitality Management. AVI Publishing Co., Westport, CT.

 Menus

College foodservices must give their customers what they want or someone off campus will. Customer satisfaction begins with menu planning. In a residence hall system, there are four steps in planning menus:

1. Establishing the menu
2. Keeping adequate records
3. Maintaining a system for feedback from students and staff to those responsible for the menus
4. Reviewing the menus and making changes

ESTABLISHING THE MENU

The old adage "variety is the spice of life" is particularly relevant to college foodservices. Boredom and monotony are constant complaints of customers who must eat the same food in the same place, prepared by the same cooks, every day.

There is not much a foodservice can do to change the cooks. What does management do, fire them every month and hire new ones? The decor in the serving line and dining room is too expensive to change every month. A little variety can be added by decorating at holidays and for special dinners. Yet there is still the basic sameness.

That leaves changing or rotating the menu as a primary way to break the monotony of a foodservice operation. The most practical way to do this is to set up cycle menus.

Cycle Menus

Most commercial restaurants have a 1-day cycle menu, with the same menu repeated every day of the week. In some, a buffet, rather than the standard menu, is offered on Sunday. Therefore, they have a 2-cycle menu, one menu being used 6 days per week and the second on the seventh day.

A few years ago, 3-week cycle menus were used by a number of colleges. With the acceptance of new ideas and the need to please customers more, many colleges now are using a 4-, 5- or 6-week cycle.

A 2- or 3-week cycle menu repeats often enough that students can remember combinations and therefore anticipate what is coming up in the next few days. When menus are spread over 4, 5 or 6 weeks, the monotony is broken for most students, but the cycle is short enough so that the menus can be repeated during the school term.

From an operational point of view, it is advantageous to repeat a menu as often as possible. The more frequently a menu is repeated, the easier and more economical it is to purchase and prepare food and to use leftovers. That is why most restaurants use the same basic menu every day.

The repeat frequency of a 5-week cycle menu is shown in Table 2.1 for a 15-week school term plus 1 week for finals, As you can see, cycle 1 is served four times and the others three times during each term.

Some schools try to make sure that cycle 1 contains the most popular menus, with well-liked items and combinations, because it is served one more time than the others. It is also the welcome menu at the beginning of the term and the one used during the stress of finals week.

The entree selection is the heart of any menu. In the past, until the late 1960s, many schools offered one entree per meal. This was the cheapest and easiest method to provide nutritious foods for students. The selection by the student was to eat or not eat. Fig. 2.1 shows a typical residence hall menu from 1955.

When liver was offered there was no need to order from the meat supplier the same portions as house count. Not everyone took an entree that night. Of those that did, only a small percentage wanted or liked it.

Schools change and in the 1970s they began offering selective menus with multiple choices of entrees, salads, desserts and beverages.

With the students' ability to make many selections it is no longer the responsibility of the schools to force students to eat nutritious meals. Instead the school can only offer well-balanced meals and try to educate students about nutritional values. Figure 2.2 exhibits a pamphlet published by the Michigan State University foodservice staff to help students better understand proper eating habits.

TABLE 2.1. The Rotation of Menus
in a 5-Week Cycle

	Menu				
Week	1	2	3	4	5
1	×				
2		×			
3			×		
4				×	
5					×
6	×				
7		×			
8			×		
9				×	
10					×
11	×				
12		×			
13			×		
14				×	
15					×
Finals	×				

Menu Planning

Setting up menus is a time-consuming and challenging task. A good method is to design different menus for each school term and use them for a couple of years, adding and subtracting a few items each year based on student responses, availability and cost of ingredients, and other considerations. After 3 or 4 years, the accumulated changes will lead to some imbalances so that a complete revision will be needed.

Some schools now offer three entrees for lunch and dinner, and use the following guidelines in menu planning:

Breakfast	Lunch	Dinner
Orange Juice	Baked Spanish Rice	Ham Loaf with Mustard
Hot and Cold Cereals	Canned Peas	and Horseradish Sauce
Scrambled Eggs	Shredded Cabbage	Scalloped Potatoes
Buttered Toast and Jam	Salad	Buttered Spinach
Coffee/Tea/Milk	Bread and Butter	Molded Peach Salad
	Fruit Cup	Bread and Butter
	Small Hermit	Ice Cream Slice
	Coffee/Tea/Milk	Coffee/Tea/Milk

FIG. 2.1.   Typical residence hall menu in fall of 1955. Note that only one entree per meal is offered.

Lunch:
  Sandwich
  Hot extender (macaroni and cheese, goulash)
  Diet plate (fruit plate, salad bowl)
Dinner:
  Solid meat (chicken, roast beef, fish)
  Hot extender (spaghetti, beef stew)
  Diet plate (fruit plate, salad bowl)

Under a board contract the dining room has a captive audience and monotony is a problem; therefore the more selections offered, the better. At the same time, too many selections can cause production problems for the kitchen and quality problems on the serving line. A happy medium is necessary.

To the three types of entrees suggested in the guidelines, a foodservice manager might consider adding hot dogs and hamburgers for every lunch. Or maybe hot dogs and hamburgers on an alternative basis, giving four entrees per day. Some schools have found that students like sandwiches in the evening and had added them to increase selections at dinner. Saturday noon might have a brunch menu or include a breakfast item (pancakes, eggs) as one of the entrees. Some schools schedule a vegetarian entree in all halls at every meal; others offer a total vegetarian menu at one hall.

Figure 2.3 shows examples of breakfast, lunch and dinner menus at Michigan State University.

The purpose of a cycle menu is to give variety to students and at the same time help the kitchen staff by repetition of menus. If a foodservice wants a 3-week cycle for kitchen ease, it can add variety by listing more entrees than it will serve. For example, suppose it offers three entrees every lunch. The master menu would list five entrees and each unit would select the three it wanted to serve.

MICHIGAN STATE UNIVERSITY
DEPARTMENT OF RESIDENCE HALLS

GOOD NUTRITION should be part of your lifestyle. The Residence Halls Food Service knows how important good nutrition is to you, as a college student living in a residence hall. Besides meeting your nutritional needs, it offers information about living better now -- and later.

CHOOSING FOOD WISELY now can really help to insure your freedom to enjoy your favorite foods for the rest of your life. Moderation now can help to lower your chances of developing such medical problems as high blood pressure, obesity, arteriosclerosis, diabetes, and elevated cholesterol levels in your blood.

MODERATION now means limiting your selection of highly salted foods like chips and processed meats (or using a salt shaker), high cholesterol foods--cheeses, red meats, butter, fried foods, alcoholic beverages, and foods with highly refined sugars--many desserts.

IMPROVING YOUR DIET is easy for the informed student. "Proper Eating," a brochure available from your food service manager, can guide you on the types and amounts of foods that you should include in your diet to maintain good health. And watch your hall's newsletter for nutritional information to help you "Keep Informed to Keep Healthy."

EXERCISE moves you toward better health. Teamed with educated food selection, exercise helps to round out a good health regimen. Exercise burns food energy (calories) without increasing your appetite and helps to prevent or lower the risk of those dietary-related diseases. Exercise increases muscle tone, gives a general sense of well-being, and can often be more energizing than a nap (but no substitute for adequate rest). Exercise can be a daily routine, even such a habit that you don't notice it until you miss a workout. It's wise to include aerobic exercise (the kind that leaves you breathless and your heart pounding) and, of course if you have had any health problems, to check with your doctor before trying strenuous routines. Remember, walking and swimming are excellent all-around exercises.

ALCOHOL consumption, a regular activity in many students' college days, can have a big impact on your nutritional pattern. You should know that alcohol is relatively high in calories--consuming 300 calories in a Friday TG would not be difficult--with minimal nutritional value. And remember those calories may be replacing nutrient-rich calories or be "extras" that simply add weight. Also, who feels like exercising after a big night out? If alcohol is part of your lifestyle, you should be wise and include it in moderation.

SNACKING, another activity common in many students' lifestyles, can be good or bad. Snacks can serve a useful purpose. From our kindergarten days--remember those cookies and milk breaks, we snack for a little extra energy to make it to our next meal. We also can snack to supplement our nutrient intake and meet our daily requirements. Or we can foolishly let snacking harm our nutritional patterns by indulging in high-calorie, low-value foods or by simply eating too much. You should be as wise in selecting and limiting your snacks as in any other part of your diet.

FIG. 2.2. Michigan State University has developed this short pamphlet to encourage good eating habits among students.

Breakfast _____ Previous Count _____ Forecast _____ Actual Count

Prunes
Assorted Fruit Juices
Assorted Dry Cereals, Granola
Cream of Wheat (as desired)
Scrambled Eggs and Bacon
Fritters, Hot Syrup
Jelly Donuts (Dozen)
Glazed Fried Cakes (Dozen)
Toast, Beverages, Condiments

Late Risers: Juice, Dry Cereals, Donuts, Beverages

Lunch _____ Previous Count _____ Forecast _____ Actual Count

____ ____ Canadian Cheese Soup, Crackers
____ ____ Baked Spaghetti
____ ____ Spartan Club Sandwich (make in kitchen)
____ ____ 1-oz Fish Sticks/Bun
____ ____ Fruit Plate

____ ____
____ ____ Tossed   ____ ____ Carrot Raisin
____ ____ Cottage Cheese   ____ ____ Fruit Cocktail with Sliced Apples
____ ____ Yogurt   ____ ____ Potato
____ ____ Strawberry Gelatin

____ ____ Chocolate Oatmeal Cookies
____ ____ Butterscotch Pudding
____ ____ Soft Serve
____ ____

Breads, Beverages. Condiments, FRUIT AVAILABLE ON REQUEST

Dinner _____ Previous Count _____ Forecast _____ Actual Count

____ ____ Wet Burritos
____ ____ Chicken Hoagie/Ponderosa Bun
____ ____ French Waffle, Hot Syrup, MSU Sausage
____ ____ Baked Sole

____ ____
____ ____ Oven-Browned Potatoes
____ ____ Winter Mixed Vegetables
____ ____ Harvard Beets
____ ____ Chicken Pilaf with Mushrooms

____ ____ Super Salad Bar   ____ ____ Macaroni
____ ____ Cottage Cheese
____ ____ Mandarin Orange Gelatin
____ ____ Applesauce

____ ____ Key Lime Pie
____ ____ Lemon Layer Cake
____ ____ Soft Serve
____ ____ Fruit in Season

Granola Bread (Each), Beverages, Condiments

WEDNESDAY   September 28   November 2   December 7   WEEK II
                                                 Finals

FIG. 2.3.   Examples of Michigan State University (MSU) menus.

Master Menu
Burritos
Baked Spaghetti
Spartan Club Sandwich
Fish Sticks on a Bun
Fruit Plate

Unit 1	Unit 2	Unit 3
Baked Spaghetti	Burritos	Burritos
Spartan Club Sandwich	Spartan Club Sandwich	Fish Sticks on a Bun
Fruit Plate	Fish Sticks on a Bun	Fruit Plate

FIG. 2.4. A cycle menu can be set up to include more entrees than are to be served; each service unit then selects those entrees it will offer. In this example, the three service units have selected three different combinations from the five entrees listed in the master menu. This is one way to add variety to cycle menus that are repeated rather often.

When the cycle repeats, each unit can either offer the same three entrees or change the selection.

Figure 2.4 illustrates how such a system might work in actual operation. From the five entrees listed in the master menu, the managers of units 1, 2 and 3 have selected three different combinations. The next time this cycle is served, they could pick different entrees. This gives variety around campus and also variety in each unit every time a particular cycle menu is offered.

Entree Frequency

For simplicity, assume that a three-cycle menu is repeated three times during a nine-week term. An Entree Frequency Chart (Fig. 2.5) will indicate at which meals each entree is served and how many times the students will see it on the serving line.

It is easy to add up each entree and multiply by three. This calculation, entered in the second to last column, shows the number of times each will be served. The right-hand column indicates how many times the students saw the menu item last year. By using L for lunch and D for dinner instead of an × it gives additional information.

Reviewing the sample frequency chart shows the following:

Burritos are both a lunch and dinner item. They are on twice as often this year as last. The purchasing department should take note that about twice as many as last year will be consumed.

Entree	Cycle 1							Cycle 2							Cycle 3							Number of times served	
	M	T	W	T	F	S	S	M	T	W	T	F	S	S	M	T	W	T	F	S	S	This year	Last year
Burritos					D										L							6	3
Fish Steak				D											D							6	9
Gyro Sandwich																				L		3	0
Hamburgers	L		L		L			L		L		L			L		L		L			27	27
Hero Sandwich																						0	3
Hot Dogs		L		L		L			L		L		L			L		L		L		27	27
Monte Cristo																				D		3	6
Roast Beef											D										D	6	3

FIG. 2.5. Frequency chart for selected entrees in 3-week cycle menu served during a 9-week term.

Fish steaks were on once per week last year for a total of nine times. This year they are on one-third less often.

Gyro sandwiches were not on last year's menu but are on for lunch, Saturday of cycle 3.

Hamburgers and hot dogs are alternated at lunch Monday through Saturday. It looks like the same as last year.

Hero sandwiches were on three times last year and taken off the menu this year. By using a chart like this, those items not on the menu are by choice, not by accident. This guide can also be used to locate a replacement item during the term.

Monte Cristo sandwiches are on half as often this year as last. Because these sandwiches are on Saturday those students going home on weekends or having a Monday through Friday meal package will not know Monte Cristos are being offered this term.

The chart shows that roast beef is similar to burritos in that it is on twice as often this year as last. The exception being roast beef is on only at dinner and burritos at both lunch and dinner.

The frequency chart shown in Fig. 2.5 is not realistic in that most schools will not serve all cycles an even three times. In more realistic 9-week terms, the first day of room and board is Monday of cycle 1; Thanksgiving recess falls on Thursday, Friday, Saturday and Sunday of cycle 1, with no foodservice on any of those days; finals end on Friday afternoon of cycle 3. The last meal for fall term is lunch on Friday. The values for the "Number of Times Served This Year" would have to be adjusted to take into account the actual school schedule. For example, burritos and fish steak would be served only five times, not six as indicated in Fig. 2.5.

In setting up a frequency chart, all entrees should be included, those being served as well as those not offered in a particular term (e.g., hero sandwiches), but likely to be used in the future. The best way to group entrees is to list them alphabetically by category, such as beef, chicken, egg, fish, lamb, pork, turkey and veal.

KEEPING ADEQUATE RECORDS

The time of year and menu combinations (the selection of items offered in a meal) are the biggest factors in how many portions of each entree are needed.

As an example, hot roast beef sandwich and a fruit plate are offered at lunch on January 16 and May 16. In many parts of the country, the cold weather in January will favor selection of the hot roast beef sandwich over the fruit plate. But the weather effect probably would not be as great in southern states as in northern ones. Differences in the weather—on a given day from one year to the next—also will affect entree selections.

The combination of menu items offered also influences how many portions of each entree are likely to be selected. If one menu is fried chicken and liver, and another is fried chicken and roast beef, a substantially higher percentage of students will select chicken when it runs against liver than when it competes with beef.

History is the best foundation for predicting which entree students will take. There will be some variation from year to year, but the best guide is what percentage of students took which entrees when they were served before.

At the end of each meal, the supervisor should record the percentage of customers that takes each item (Fig. 2.6). This should be done just before any runouts occur, not necessarily at the end of the meal. To understand why, suppose roast beef is running at 60% and chicken at 40% during a meal. With a half hour left to serve, the roast beef runs out. Obviously, all customers after this time have to take chicken; by meal's end, the percentages might be an even 50–50. In any case, the roast beef percentage would be less at the end of the meal than it was before the supply of beef ran out. The information in this chart (Fig. 2.6) is an excellent tool to be used when forecasting food preferences.

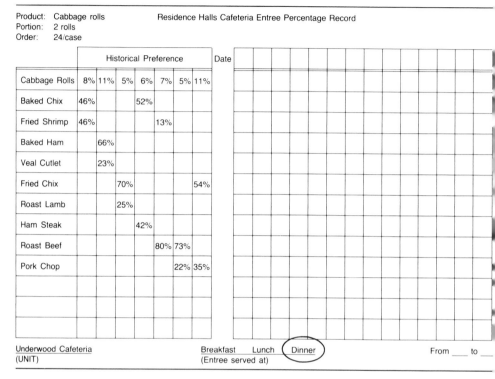

Product: Cabbage rolls   Residence Halls Cafeteria Entree Percentage Record
Portion: 2 rolls
Order: 24/case

	Historical Preference							Date
Cabbage Rolls	8%	11%	5%	6%	7%	5%	11%	
Baked Chix	46%			52%				
Fried Shrimp	46%			13%				
Baked Ham		66%						
Veal Cutlet		23%						
Fried Chix			70%			54%		
Roast Lamb		25%						
Ham Steak			42%					
Roast Beef				80%	73%			
Pork Chop					22%	35%		

Underwood Cafeteria   Breakfast   Lunch   (Dinner)   From ___ to ___
(UNIT)   (Entree served at)

FIG. 2.6.   Historical entree percentage record for cabbage rolls served in a residence hall cafeteria.

MAINTAINING A SYSTEM FOR FEEDBACK

To know what customers like and dislike, the person or committee responsible for menu planning has to use a feedback system. Casual observation and a phone call or two are not enough.

The first step in this system is from customers to the foodservice manager of each unit. A complaint form and suggestion box in the dining room and a student food committee can aid communications between students and the management. The foodservice manager should talk to students on a daily basis in the dining room and attend hall government meetings.

The information obtained in these ways should be coupled with personal observations and sent to the central management (Fig. 2.7). The complaints and comments received from all units provide the basis for evaluating menus throughout the entire foodservice operation.

REVIEWING MENUS AND MAKING CHANGES

Each week the menu committee should review the concerns of both students and staff from the previous week. This committee assesses each problem and decides one of three things:

1. It is a minor concern that requires no changes in the menu.
2. The problem is not major but should be taken into account next year at menu-planning time.
3. Due to the nature of the problem (student dislike, production problems, product unavailability, etc.), the next time this cycle is repeated the item should be changed.

Based on its review, the committee may recommend specific menu changes (Fig. 2.8).

Menus are an ever-changing part of a school foodservice. Each year a new group of students descends on the campus. In a residence hall operation or a snack shop that primarily caters to students, there is a total turnover of customers

---

WEEKLY MENU EVALUATION

TERM: F W̲ S   Date ___January 19_____
CYCLE: 1 2̲ 3 4   Unit ___Underwood Cafeteria___

Lunch
Saturday: We had four notes in the suggestion box stating that students are tired of plain old scrambled eggs.

Disjointed chicken runs us over our precosted budget.

Dinner
Monday: Too many deep fat fried items on the menu.

Friday: We had to bake the country fried steaks longer than the standardized recipe indicates.

General Comments

Signed *Margaret Power*
Foodservice Manager

FIG. 2.7. Weekly evaluation memo prepared by foodservice unit manager for the central management.

TO: Unit Managers
FROM: Menu Committee
SUBJECT: Winter Term Menu, Cycle 2

The Menu Committee has made the following recommendations and suggestions for Cycle 2 when it is repeated:

Sunday dinner: Add omelet of your choice. Replace pepper steak with seafood crepes.
Monday dinner: Change french fries to hash browns.
Tuesday lunch: Offer syrup with the Monte Cristo sandwich.
Friday dinner: Increase baking time on country fried steaks to 2–2.5 hours. Change knockwurst to quarter-pound hot dogs.
Saturday brunch: Change scrambled eggs to scrambled egg bake with ham. Offer choice of buns with Deli sandwich instead of flat bread. Drop disjointed chicken.

FIG. 2.8.   Memo prepared by menu committee recommending changes in a cycle menu.

every 4 years. If menus are to remain appealing to the changing preferences of a changing clientele, management must constantly review, evaluate and make adjustments.

REFERENCES

ANON. 1978. Sugar 'n spice—and everything nice? (or, Why you should consider capping your sweet tooth). Harvard Med. School Health Letter 4(2).

ANON. 1979. Dietary fiber. Contemporary Nutrition 4(9). Food and Nutrition Board, National Academy of Sciences, Washington, DC.

CHURCH, C. F. and CHURCH, H. N. 1970. Food Values of Portions Commonly Used. 11th Edition. J. B. Lippincott, Philadelphia, PA.

CLYDESDALE, F. M. and FRANCES, F. J. 1977. Food, Nutrition and You. Prentice-Hall, Englewood Cliffs, NJ.

DEUTSCH, R. M. 1976. Realities of Nutrition. Bull Publishing Co., Palo Alto, CA.

DWYER, J. 1979. Vegetarianism. Contemporary Nutrition 4(6). Food and Nutrition Board, National Academy of Sciences, Washington, DC.

ECKSTEIN, E. 1983. Menu Planning. 3rd Edition. AVI Publishing Co., Westport, CT.

FDA. 1974. Nutrition Labeling Terms You Should Know. HEW Publ. (FDA) 74-2010. U.S. Dept. Health and Human Services, Washington, DC.

GUSSOW, J. D. 1979. Why we need dietary guidelines, CNI Weekly Report 9(46), 4.

HANSON, G. R. and SORENSON, A. W. 1979. Nutritional Quality Index of Foods. AVI Publishing Co., Westport, CT.

MARIO, T. 1978. Quantity Cooking. AVI Publishing Co., Westport, CT.

MINOR, L. J. 1983. Nutritional Standards. AVI Publishing Co., Westport, CT.

NAS. 1980. Recommended Dietary Allowances. 9th Edition. Food and Nutrition Board, National Research Council. National Academy of Sciences, Washington, DC.

ROBERTSON, L., SLINDERS, C., and GODFREY, B. 1976. Laurel's Kitchen: Handbook for Vegetarian Cookery and Nutrition. Nilgiri Press, Berkeley, CA.

SCALA, J. 1974. Fiber—the forgotten nutrient. Food Technol. *28*, 34.

SMITH, E. B. 1975. A guide to good eating the vegetarian way. J. Nutr. Ed. *7*, 109.

STEPHENSON, M. 1978. The confusing world of health foods. FDA Consumer (HEW Publ. 79–2108), July–August.

USDA. 1977. Food for Fitness—A Daily Food Guide. Leaflet 424. U.S. Dept. of Agriculture, Agriculture Research Service, Washington, DC.

USDA. 1980. Nutrition and Your Health—Dietary Guidelines for Americans. U.S. Government Printing Office, Washington, DC.

U.S. SENATE SELECT COMMITTEE ON NUTRITION AND HUMAN NEEDS. 1977. Dietary Goals for the United States. 2nd Edition. U.S. Government Printing Office, Washington, DC.

WATT, B. K. and MERRILL, A. L. 1963. Composition of Foods. Agriculture Handbook No. 8. U.S. Dept. of Agriculture, Washington, DC.

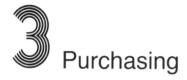 Purchasing

Purchasing for any foodservice operation is a necessary evil. It is complicated, the logistics are difficult and, probably the worst part, it is time-consuming.

Foodservice managers are confronted with a multitude of immediate problems—a sick cook, a broken dish machine, tardy student employees, soup that is too salty, fish that did not get thawed, a union steward who wants to talk about the grievance submitted yesterday. Oh, and another thing, ever so small—the food orders have to be placed.

In a small school, the foodservice manager has to test products, set specifications, talk to sales people, take inventories, design menus, determine needs, do price comparisons, write orders, receive the goods and then pay the invoices. A larger school with more financial resources can afford specialized staff to handle some of these duties and may operate a warehouse as part of a centralized-purchasing system.

ADVANTAGES OF CENTRALIZED PURCHASING

The two primary reasons for a school to construct and operate a centralized-purchasing warehouse are to save money and to increase the convenience and efficiency of operations. However, centralized purchasing through a campus-owned facility is not suitable for all schools. Although the construction costs of a well-designed food warehouse may be recouped many times over by reductions in expenses, the savings possible in any given situation depend on several factors.

The size of the school is the key to savings associated with a centralized facility. A school with an enrollment of 10,000 or less would save little by operating its own warehouse because any reduction in purchasing costs would be outweighed by the cost to build, maintain and staff the facility.

One of the main questions asked by schools is what student population justifies a warehouse. Unfortunately, I cannot give an exact figure. However, we can gain some understanding of the issue by considering commercial firms.

As commercial wholesale firms grow in size, they can spread their overhead costs over larger sales dollars and sell their products with less markup than in the past. It is much the same in the institutional field as in the retail: The big are getting bigger and the small are going out of business. In order to survive, wholesalers have to grow. This gives wholesalers—whether retail or institutional—more purchasing power, and therefore they can buy cheaper. At the same time, sales are greater and the markup can be reduced and still cover overhead.

One stimulus for the growth of commercial wholesalers is the increased preference of customers for "one-stop shopping." When delivery expenses for new trucks, gas, repairs and labor start to climb, companies must devise ways to increase their income in order to cover their rising expenses. If a firm is selling staples, it would not be enough to sell an extra case or two per delivery. That would not generate enough to cover climbing costs. The best strategy for increasing revenue would be to increase the product line.

Why not deliver ten cases of paper items along with the canned goods? If the firm added a freezer to its warehouse, many additional items could be offered to customers, including frozen fruits, vegetables, meats, fish, poultry and frozen entrees. Warehouse costs would go up, but so would sales and the cost of delivery would stay about the same.

Several lessons for campus-based warehouse facilities can be learned from the experience of commercial firms. First, such a facility must be large enough to generate substantial savings in the purchase of goods and, in turn, to allow reductions in prices charged to customers. Second, the facility should be designed to handle as many different kinds of items as is feasible. This will have the effect of spreading delivery expenses over a larger number of items and may permit a foodservice to offer new menu items that might stimulate sales. And finally, a campus-based facility must be designed and staffed for efficient operation so that purchasing savings are not eaten up by increased labor costs, spoilage or pilfering.

The second reason a school might consider building a warehouse is the convenience of having a supply of goods on campus. This is especially relevant for schools, both large and small, located miles from any supplier. If a school does not have at least two large suppliers close by, it may well benefit by building its own warehouse. If there is only one supplier in the area, the school may have trouble obtaining the products it wants. The supplier may talk a good game but chances are service, products and pricing are not what they would be if two or more suppliers were competing for the school's business. Even when the number of suppliers near a school is limited, the school must be of a certain minimum size to warrant the cost of a warehouse operation.

A small school located away from a major metropolitan area and with only small wholesale houses to supply its needs is going to have trouble. It is too small to economically operate a campus-based warehouse, but its suppliers are likely to charge fairly high prices, provide mediocre service and not want to supply products the school needs.

CENTRAL-WAREHOUSE AND DIRECT-DELIVERY SYSTEMS

A number of schools have set up semi-warehouse systems. For example, when some residence halls or other buildings were constructed, larger-than-normal basements were included. Such items as canned goods, soaps and waxes, paper goods and some small kitchen equipment are warehoused in these large basements. Other units on campus order these items from the on-campus stores and order meat, produce, dairy goods, etc., from local suppliers. As some schools grew the system expanded to a central warehousing concept.

Central Warehousing

Soon after World War II, Michigan State University opened a building designed solely as a foodservice warehouse. During the university's growth spurt in the early 1960s, Robert Herron, former food stores manager, designed a new facility, which opened in the spring of 1964 (Fig. 3.1).

Including the fast-food snack shop operation, the number of meals served at Michigan State University is estimated to be 70,000 per day, large enough to warrant a warehouse. It is estimated that the warehouse operation saves the university about $1 million per year in the cost of food and related items. Yearly sales for Food Stores is in the area of $10 million.

The University of Virginia and Central Michigan University, two schools about the same size—16,000 students with 6,000 living in residence halls—are handling their food purchasing in two different ways.

University of Virginia

In the early 1980s the University of Virginia opened a warehouse operation [see Fontana and Ordell (1983)]. The university's foodservice department pro-

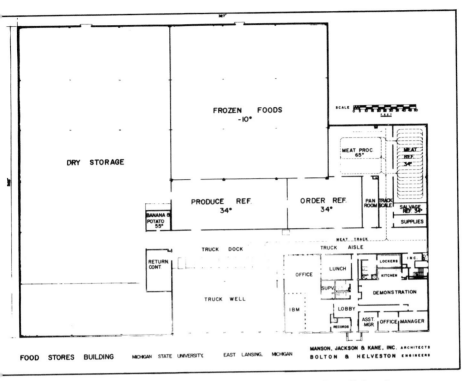

FIG. 3.1.   Floor plan of Food Stores Building at Michigan State University.

vides meals and refreshments to a student body of 16,400 through three cafeterias, six snack bars, a sweet shop, two convenience grocery stores, a vending
service, a catering service, concessions and a rathskeller–pub. In addition, it has
a faculty luncheon club and a post-graduate hotel dining facility.

In 1977 the university began planning and a site search for a 44,000-ft^2 facility
to replace the decentralized foodservice support system that had evolved over the
years. In the end, a 15-year-old manufacturing plant, containing 64,800 ft^2 was
purchased and converted into a modern food-processing facility (Fig. 3.2). The
Food Service Central Support Facility—or as it is known, the Food Center—
began operations in August 1982. It has three functions: warehousing, processing and distribtuion.

The warehousing operation is responsbile for receiving, storing and reissuing
all food stuffs and supplies. (Milk and bread, however, are delivered directly to
individual serving units by the vendors.) In the dock area, products are counted
and inspected by trained personnel. Many products are weighed on an automatic
digital scale, which records the weight, tare and date and prints a ticket for

FOOD CENTER

University of Virginia
Food Service Division

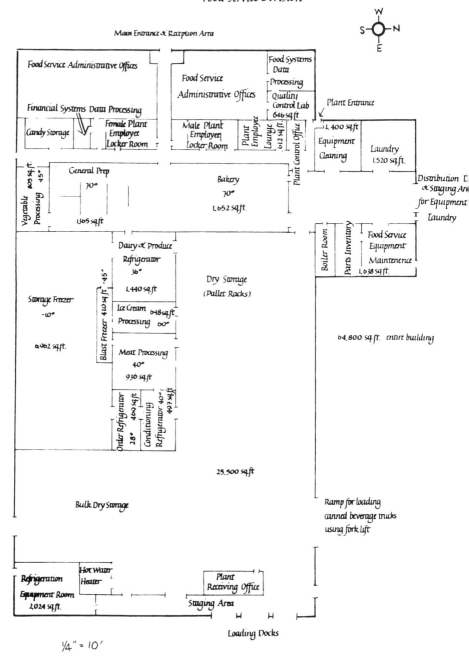

FIG. 3.2.   Floor plan of Food Center at University of Virginia. This facility contains nearly 33,400 ft² of storage space plus ample room for food processing and preparation.

accounting purposes. This scale can weigh full pallets which are then moved into storage by electrically powered equipment.

Storage space of 33,902 ft² is allocated to dry, refrigerated and frozen products. The dry storage area can accommodate a 180-day reserve of food. Four high pallet racking and two bulk storage areas are used. Steam heaters are used to protect the products from freezing. The freezer, maintained at −10°F is designed for high-density bulk-storage, utilizing narrow aisles and drive-in pallet racking. Other refrigerated facilities include a 40°F conditioning refrigerator, a 28°F order assembly area and a −40°F blast freezer.

The Food Center delivers processed foods and warehoused items daily to 21 user units at 15 different locations. The delivery fleet consists of one 22-ft truck and two 18-ft trucks, one of which has refrigerator and freezer capabilities. In addition, 12 vending route trucks are serviced from the central facility through a separate access way.

Food-processing areas are separated from storage areas by prefabricated insulated panel walls. Doors are electrically timed or equipped with air screens to control the atmosphere in critical areas. Two sophisticated computer systems monitor inventory levels, compute purchasing forecasts and print requisitions tailored to the warehouse layout.

The food production area is divided into a number of units: meat processing, bakery, vegetable processing, ice cream making and general preparation (e.g., sandwiches for vending machines). In addition a quality control laboratory and equipment cleaning room are located near the production units.

High rates of food production are attained with the modern commercial equipment installed in the processing units. This, in turn, permits considerable flexibility in staffing. For example, the meal products required for one week can be produced in 3 days, so the meat staff can be assigned to ice cream production or general preparation work during the rest of the week. Also, year-round production is feasible with employees scheduled during student vacations to mass-produce products that can be frozen and held for use when school is in session.

It is anticipated that the Food Center will make possible increased efficiencies and cost savings in the purchasing, processing and distribtuion of food at the University of Virginia. It is more convenient than the old system, since it brings all foodservice operations—including administrative and support services—under one roof.

Central Michigan University

In the early 1950s, Central Michigan University set up what might be called a half-and-half purchasing/warehousing system. The foodservice department operated a full-fledged meatshop and bakery. At that time commercial suppliers could not provide the types and quantities of products required by the university foodservice units. In addition, an inconvenient basement warehouse stored canned goods and paper goods. In this system, individual units ordered some items directly from local suppliers and some from the foodservice's central stores operation.

In the early 1970s, the university raised concerns about the cost and efficiency of the warehousing operation. At that time, the foodservice department was responsible for providing meals to 6,000+ students in five residence halls (total school enrollment was about 16,000 students) and for providing fast-food, public cafeteria and banquet service at the University Center. James Reath, manager of University Food Services, conducted a study to determine which of three options would be most cost effective: (1) continuation of the current half-and-half system; (2) construction of an expanded, modern warehousing/processing facility; or (3) use of commercial wholesalers to deliver all items directly to each unit.

A small-scale test of a direct delivery system, involving one unit, was conducted to assess its feasibility and to answer many of the questions about the selection and quality of goods, dependability of deliveries, storage capabilities in units and out-of-stocks.

The results indicated that a one-vendor, direct-delivery system would have the following advantages:

1. Permanently reduced labor needs for the central stores operation
2. Lower inventories in units and in the central warehouse
3. Savings in utilities, equipment and maintenance for the central stores area
4. Possibly better utilization of space
5. More frequent and detailed reports on purchasing and usage of items

At the conclusion of this study, the decision was made to eliminate the central stores operation and award the bid of grocery items to one major supplier. Once the new system was underway throughout Central Michigan University, the anticipated benefits became clearer. The most important of these, in terms of cost savings, was the reduced inventory that was carried with the new system. For example, in the fall of 1976 before the direct-delivery system was instituted, the total inventory for both the central stores operation and the individual units was $485,000. In contrast, in April 1979, the total foodservice inventory was less than $40,000. In fact, the new system operates with a ''negative'' inventory if one considers that the groceries in the units are consumed before the bills are paid.

In a direct-delivery, one-vendor system, the major supplier acts, in effect, as a warehouse for the purchaser. This type of system has become feasible in recent years because of changes in commercial food processing and distribution. For example, many items (boxed beef, precut pork chops, bulk ground beef, hamburger patties) that were unavailable from commercial firms 20 years ago are now commonplace.

As mentioned earlier in this chapter, many warehousing firms have diversified and expanded their facilities in recent years so they can handle anything from steaks to canned beans to cleaning supplies.

DIFFERENCES BETWEEN UNIVERSITY-OWNED AND COMMERCIAL WAREHOUSES

There are both similarities and differences between a university-owned warehouse and a commercial warehouse. In general, operating costs can be lower for an institutional warehouse than for a commercial one; this difference should translate into cost savings for a college foodservice. On the other hand, many of the policies and practices associated with wholesale purchasing are the same for both commercial and university operations. Some of these are discussed in the following section.

The major difference between a commercial operation and a college operation is the underlying objective. A commercial firm is in business to make a profit. But a nonprofit warehouse run by a school only need break even; its primary goal is not profit but service.

A school warehouse provides many services to individual units that a commercial firm would not, for example, providing specified items, portion sizes, packs, grades, etc., that a particular unit wants.

A central warehouse handles purchasing for all units in a foodservice. Without such central buying, each unit would probably have to hire an additional person to talk to salespeople, run cuttings, do comparison shopping, place orders, check in goods and make payments to vendors.

Warehouse trucks can be loaned to units to move equipment, furniture and dance floors. Warehouse computers can be programmed for menu precosting or analysis of food and labor costs.

The first concern of a buyer for a school warehouse is whether something is a good deal for the school. A buyer in a commercial firm considers whether it is a good deal for the wholesaler. Although in the commercial operation it may turn out to also be a good deal for customers, that is not the primary consideration for the buyer. Both commercial and institutional buyers think ''is it a good deal for us?'' The *us*, however, has two different meanings.

Operating Expenses

A major operating expense for a commercial firm is its sales force. In contrast, a campus facility does not need five or six salespeople to go from unit to unit selling products and taking orders. Eliminating those people and the backup staff that is needed to keep them on the road substantially reduces expenses.

Delivery expenses are also different for the two operations. A single campus, or even one with a satellite or two, has a shorter radius of distribution than does a commercial operator. A warehouse located on the outskirts of campus may have to make deliveries 2 or 3 miles away; a commercial operator would laugh at that small figure.

A small wholesaler, for example, may have to cover a 200- to 400-square-mile area compared with a college campus of 1 to 8 square miles. Large wholesalers may travel 250 to 300 miles before making their first delivery of the day. A campus operation can make five or six stops in that same time, with savings in gas, oil, tire wear, and general truck maintenance.

A campus warehouse also has lower inventory costs than does a commercial firm. The foodservice warehouse at Michigan State University carries two china and two stainless steel patterns for 23 different cafeterias. A commercial firm may have to carry inventory with as many different patterns as customers it serves.

The same holds true for fruits and vegetables, an example being yellow cling peaches. Michigan State University stocks one size, one grade (Choice Grade, 30–35 count in light syrup). A commercial wholesaler would have to stock three or four different kinds to meet the needs of its different customers. A country club might need a Fancy Grade A in two sizes, nursing homes the 40–50 count in water or light syrup, a truck stop the 25–30 count in heavy syrup but a Standard Grade.

Taxes are another expense borne by commercial operations that nonprofit schools do not have to worry about. Schools do not pay federal, state, county or city taxes on land, buildings or income. In addition, colleges and universities do not pay sales taxes when they buy desks for offices, typewriters, construction materials or trucks. Nor do they pay taxes on the gas and oil for those trucks.

WHOLESALE PURCHASING

In the last section, some of the differences between institutional and commercial wholesale operations were discussed. This section focuses on how they resemble each other. For all practical purposes, a campus-based warehouse operates in exactly the same way as does a commercial wholesale firm. Both buy directly from manufacturers or through brokerage firms; both must contend with the usual practices and policies found in the food business.

To be eligible to buy on a direct basis from companies, purchasers must order large quantities. Some companies accept orders for 500 to 1,000 lb of goods, but a 3,000- to 5,000-lb minimum is more typical. Other companies require a 10,000-lb minimum order, and a few even have truckload minimums ranging from 36,000 to 40,000 lb.

Thirty-day credit is commonly extended to wholesalers by vendors. However, meat companies want their money in 7 days, and produce companies at terminals ask for cash at the time of pickup.

Discounts for quick payment are readily available to both commercial and institutional wholesalers. The most common is *2% 10, net 30.* That means if the bill is paid within 10 days, a 2% discount can be deducted from the payment. If the purchaser cannot, or does not want to make payment within 10 days, then payment is due within 30 days. No discount is allowed after 10 days.

Free-on-board (F.0.B.)—a common term used in the wholesale food industry—specifies who is going to pay shipping costs and from where. *F.0.B. destination* indicates that the price of the product includes all shipping charges. For example, if a case of peaches cost $20 F.0.B. destination, the purchaser would be charged $20 per case delivered to its warehouse. *F.0.B. plant or factory* indicates that the peaches would cost the buyer $20 *plus* freight charges from the plant to the warehouse. Another variation might be *F.0.B. Chicago warehouse.* The case of peaches, grown and processed in California, would cost $20 plus freight from Chicago to the buyer's warehouse. The $20 includes the freight cost from California to Chicago; the buyer has to pay only the freight from Chicago.

Generally, when freight is separate (F.0.B. plant) from the purchase price, the 2% 10 discount does not apply to the freight charge. When the freight is included (F.0.B. destination) in the price quoted by the packer, the discount can be taken by the wholesaler. This is illustrated in Table 3.1.

The 3-cent difference between F.0.B. destination and F.0.B. plant in the example in Table 3.1 does not look like much, but for every truckload of peaches it would save the wholesaler about $20. Add that to the $270 discount received for paying the bill in 10 days, and it would not take very many truckloads to save $1000. A college-based wholesale operation should not ignore such savings.

Company Salespeople and Brokerage Firms

Wholesalers, both university owned and commercial, buy their goods either through company salespeople or through brokerage firms. It is estimated that

TABLE 3.1. Free-on-Board Cost Comparison

Item	Case price	Transportation	Price	Less 2% 10	Wholesaler's net cost
F.O.B. destination Peaches	$21.50	Included	$21.50	0.43	$21.07
F.O.B. plant Peaches	$20.00	$1.50	$21.50	0.40	$21.10

each system accounts for about half of all food sales in the United States. To illustrate the differences between company salespeople and brokerage firms, let us examine two hypothetical cases: a large cereal company in Battle Creek, Michigan, and a small company selling fish in Massachusetts.

The cereal company is large enough and does enough business in every state to justify a sales force of 50 people. Each state is assigned its own salesperson who visits wholesalers and tries to sell them the cereal company's products. This person is on the company's payroll—paid on salary, on commission, or on a combination of both. Whatever the method of payment, company salespeople are familiar with and promote only the products of the company that employs them.

In contrast, the fish company in Massachusetts cannot afford 50 salespeople on its payroll; it cannot even afford 25 (one for every two states). In order to frequently call on wholesale houses throughout the country, a small company like this contracts with a brokerage firm to represent the company.

A *broker* is an independent sales agent who negotiates contracts of purchase and sale for a fee or commission. A brokerage house represents a number of firms and each firm may manufacture a variety of products. A brokerage firm receives a commission, usually 1–8% of every sale made in the territory assigned to it by the *principal,* the person or company from whom an agent's authority derives.

In our example, the Massachusetts fish company is the principal to the brokerage firm and assigns a territory to that firm. It might be a city or maybe half a state; in less populated areas, a territory might comprise a whole state or even two states. The cost to the fish company of contracting with a brokerage house is much less than the cost of maintaining a company sales staff. On the other hand, the brokerage firm's sales staff is less knowledgeable about the fish company's products than company salespeople would be. When brokers for the fish company walk into customers' offices, they have to decide which of the 500 or so products that they represent should be discussed. A lot of times it is not the fish company's items.

After a food brokerage firm has been hired, the principal must train the brokers about its products. What does the company manufacture or process? How is it packed? How should it be prepared? Is it designed for all types of feeding or just for fancy restaurants? What is the selling price? Is it F.O.B. plant or destination? The principal may travel with the broker's sales staff for a time to help promote and explain the products to wholesalers. If a company thinks that a brokerage firm is doing an inadequate sales job, it may fire the broker and negotiate a contract with another brokerage firm.

Both systems, company salespersons and brokerage firms, have advantages and disadvantages to manufacturers. The advantage of company salespeople is that they are not trying to sell hundreds of different items every time they call on a customer; the disadvantage is the high cost of maintaining a sales staff on the road. The advantage to the manufacturer of using brokerage firms is the lower cost of covering a wide territory; the disadvantage is that a broker has less knowledge of and less time to spend on selling a company's products.

Large Brokerage Firms

The Pfeister Company, with its main offices in Detroit, is used to illustrate a large brokerage firm. It presently has a sales force of 135 people with a clerical staff of 25. Its area of distribution, or potential market, contains 12 to 13 million people. It has branch offices in two other Michigan cities, Saginaw and Grand Rapids. Out-of-state offices are in Toledo, Ohio, and Fort Wayne, Indiana.

Organizationally it is divided into two main divisions—retail, which is 85% of its volume, covered by 121 salespeople, and foodservice, with a staff of 14. Each division is broken down into workable units. This allows each salesperson to become more of a specialist and cover only one section of the industry.

Foodservice (15%)
    Dry
    Frozen
    Industrial/Food Processors
Retail (85%)
    Confectionary/Snacks
    General Merchandise
    Grocery
    Health and Beauty Aids
    Perishable–Frozen/Produce–Dairy/Deli/Meat

Table 3.2 outlines the principals, their general product lines and the year Pfeister Food Service was appointed to represent them.

The retail division and its principals are listed in Table 3.3. (see pp. 54–57).

Small Brokerage Firms

Most small brokerage firms start when a salesperson working for a brokerage company decides, for one reason or another, to branch out on his or her own. Normally they start by representing from one to three principals and expand as they can.

In other cases it is two salespeople from either the same brokerage firm or maybe from different firms that decide to go into business for themselves. Normally they start in someone's home, using their personal phone and either using an answering machine or their spouse as a secretary. After a few years, when business has grown, a permanent office staff is hired and an office is rented. Some small firms expand into large corporations, such as Pfeister, or by design stay small.

As an example, Spaulding Sales, Inc., located in the Detroit area, is being

TABLE 3.2.   Pfeister Foodservice Principals

Principal	Product lines	Date appointed
Alex Foods	Salad bar items, slaw and potato salad	1983
American Home Foods	Chef Boy-ar-dee entrees, mustard, soups	1963
R. C. Bigelow, Inc.	Regular and herbal teas	1982
California Almond Growers Exchange	Blue Diamond snacks and industrial almonds	1963
California Valley Marketing	Tri-Valley fruits, vegetable and tomato products	1970
Castle and Cooke Foods	Dole pineapple/Bumblebee seafoods	1935
Chicopee, Inc.	Cleaning cloths, aprons	1983
Dalgety Foods	Frozen bulk fruits and vegetables	1954
Drakes Batter Mix	Coatings, cake mixes	1970
Frionor Norwegian Frozen Fish, Inc.	Fish fillets, portions, school products	1971
Kentucky Sausage	Patties, links, specialty pork items	1982
Kronos Foods	Specialty Greek foods, gyros, pita bread	1982
McIlhenny Company	Tabasco sauce, Bloody Mary mix	1926
3-M Company	Foodservice cleaning pads, grill screens	1973
Pierce/Marketeam	Pre-cooked specialty chicken products	1962
Readi-Bake, Inc.	Frozen cookie dough, breads, rolls	1976
Rich Seapak Corporation	Shrimp, specialty fish, vegetable items	1977
Rogers Walla Walla, Inc.	Frozen french fries	1967
Sanna—Div. of Beatrice Foods	Hot cocoa mix/puddings	1976
J. M. Smucker Company/Dickinson	Jams, jellies, ice cream toppings	1978
Stouffer Foods Corporation	Frozen entrees, side dishes, bases	1980
Sugar Foods Corporation	Sugar and salt substitutes	1982
Sun-Diamond Growers of California	Walnut, raisins, prune products	1929
Treesweet Products Company	Canned and frozen juices	1934
Zartic Meat, Inc.	Frozen raw and breaded meat specialties	1983

used to illustrate a small brokerage firm. It is a family-owned operation. The father started the business in 1965 representing four companies. Today they represent 16 principals selling to about 75 customers. The staff consists of three street salespeople: the father, his son and daughter. A street salesperson is one that makes direct sales (visits) to clients. Backup staff consists of two office personnel and a part-time, in-house sales force. In-house sales is done over the telephone.

Competitive Bidding

Many college foodservices contract for goods based on competitive bids. Private schools without state funding may use a different system. A state-supported school must develop written specifications for the items it wants and then

Michigan State University — REQUEST FOR QUOTATION

NO. 1954

DATE: JUNE 10, 1987

1.
J. Duckett Corp.
1125 Hunters Lane
Blank City, USA

2.
E. Reneaud Corp.
207 Alaskan Highway
Blank City, USA

3.
E. Schnieder Corp.
1412 Twin Road
Blank City, USA

ADDRESS REPLY TO:
MICHIGAN STATE UNIVERSITY
PURCHASING DEPARTMENT
PURCHASING BUILDING
EAST LANSING, MICH. 48824

INSTRUCTIONS FOR BIDDERS

1. Submit quotations on this form only.
2. If substitutes are offered attach or write on this form full specifications.
3. If a better price can be offered by slightly changing quantities requested please advise and quote on that amount.
4. Unless otherwise stated, there is no restriction on the quantities that may be ordered, either more or less.
5. All prices will be considered F.O.B. destination unless otherwise indicated. If prices are quoted F.O.B. shipping point, please indicate total transportation charges.
6. Unless otherwise noted by the vendor, prices quoted are firm and this bid will be considered open for a period of 45 days from due date noted.
7. This inquiry implies no obligation on the part of the buyer. This is not an order.
8. In case of default by vendor, M.S.U. Purchasing Department may procure the articles or services from other sources and hold the vendor responsible for any excess cost occasioned thereby which includes loss of research time.

QUOTATION DUE BY: August 14, 1987

RETURN TO ATTENTION: D. Ziolkowski

NOTE
FOR QUESTIONS RE BID
PH. 517-353-2977

ITEM	QUANTITY	UNIT	DESCRIPTION	NET UNIT PRICE	TOTAL AMOUNT
1.	150	cs	Peaches Diced - Yellow Cling - U.S. Choice Light Syrup 6/10		
2.	800	cs	Peaches - Sliced - Yellow Cling - U.S. Choice Light Syrup 6/10		
3.	400	cs	Fruit Cocktail - U.S. Choice Light Syrup 6/10		

BUYERS C & O SIDING   ALL PRODUCTS 1987 PACK

MAIL IN ENCLOSED WHITE ENVELOPE

DELIVERY WEEK OF SEPTEMBER 28, 1987........

VENDOR ID NO.	CHECK IF APPLICABLE ☐ MINORITY BUS. ☐ SMALL BUS.		TOTAL	
PRICES F.O.B. FOOD STORES	SHIPMENT PROMISE AFTER RECEIPT OF ORDER ___ DAYS	SUGGEST BEST WAY TO SHIP		
TERMS	YOUR QUOTATION NO	QUOTED BY (SIGNATURE)		DATE

NOTICE TO ALL SUPPLIERS: On April 18, 1969 the Board of Trustees of Michigan State University adopted a policy of requiring proof of equal employment practices from all University suppliers. Effective November 19, 1969 the following non-discrimination clause is hereby incorporated into and made a part of all request for quotations and purchase orders issued by Michigan State University:
  The supplier in bidding and/or filling a purchase order agrees not to discriminate against any employee or applicant for employment, with respect to hire, tenure, terms, conditions or privileges of employment, or any matter directly or indirectly related to employment, because of race, color, religion, national origin or ancestry. The supplier further agrees that every subcontractor or order given for the supplying of this order will contain a provision requiring non-discrimination in employment, as herein specified. This covenant is required pursuant to Section 4 of Act No. 251, Public Acts of the State of Michigan of 1955 as amended and any breach thereof may be regarded as a material breach of the contract or purchase order.

MSU is an Affirmative Action/Equal Opportunity Institution

FIG. 3.3. Request for quotation for canned peaches. In this example the request is to be sent to three vendors. The use of preprinted forms facilitates preparation of requests for quotations and assures that all necessary information is included.

TABLE 3.3.   Pfeister Retail Principals

Principal	Product lines	Date appointed
a. Confectionery/snacks		
California Almond Growers	Blue Diamond Vac Tin almonds, pistachios, macadamia nuts	1963
Holland American Wafer Co.	Dutch twin breads (vend only)	1982
Mauna Loa Macadamia Nut Co.	Mauna Loa Macadamia Nuts	1972
Shari Candies Inc. Div. Barg & Foster	Shari packaged candy	1981
Sun-Diamond Growers of California	Sun-Maid nature snacks and raisins	1929
Whitman's Chocolates	Whitman's Samplers and candy bars	1983
b. General merchandise		
Alabaster Industries	Alabaster Plastic Products	1979
Belmont Industries	Wrangler Jockey Underwear	1983
Blue Coral Corp.	Blue Coral car care products	1983
Contexx, Div. Leath, McCarthy & Maynard	Soft goods—towels, dish cloths, etc.	1983
Converting, Inc.	Disposable tablecloths	1979
Dart Container (nonfood trade only)	Dart foam cups	1983
Esselte-Pendaflex Corp.	Dymo & Primark store pricing system	1980
Fuji Photo—U.S.A., Inc.	Fuji film and photo products	1978
Fuld & Co.	Greeting cards	1982
Keyes Fibre, Chinet Div.	Chinet paper plates, napkins and plastic silverware	1981
Parker Pen Co., Inc.	Parker writing instruments	1983
St. Regis—School, Home & Office Products	School, home and office supplies	1982
The Bonneau Company	Bonneau and Polaroid sunglasses	1981
Transtech Industries	P/L & Packer Label Hosiery	1983
Union Carbide Corp.	Prestone products	1983
Universal Synthetic Associates, Inc. (USA)	Synthetic motor oil and additives	1983
Whitestone Products	P/L and generic disposable diapers	1981
c. Grocery		
Alpha Sales Company	Helping Hand or generic rock salt	1983
California Almond Growers Exchange	Blue Diamond almonds, pistachios and macadamia nuts	1963
California Valley Marketing	Private label fruit	1969
Campbell Sales Company	Recipe dog food	1971
	Swanson canned meat and poultry products	
Castle & Cooke Foods	Dole pineapple juice & pineapple Bumble Bee tuna, salmon & oysters	1936
Chicago Supply, Inc.	Featherweight diet foods	1983
Chicopee, Inc.	Household wipes, cleaning and dust cloths	1983
Coca-Cola Company Foods Div.	Hi-C drinks, Minute Maid lemonade crystals	1983
Dart Container	Dart foam cups	1969
Diamond Crystal Salt Co.	Diamond table, de-icing and water softener salt	1983
Doric Foods Corp.	Sunny Delight citrus drinks	1983

TABLE 3.3. (*Continued*)

Principal	Product lines	Date appointed
c. *Grocery (continued)*		
Drake's Batter Mix Company	Drake's crispy fry mix	1980
Faygo Beverages Inc.	Faygo regular and diet beverages	1982
R. T. French Company	French's mustards, potatoes, sauces and gravy mixes, seasonings, spices, pet treats and Bully Bowl cleaner	1975
Henri's Food Products Company	Henri's salad and reduced calorie dressings, Yogonaise and Yogowhip	1980
Heublein Inc.	A-1 sauce, Snap-E-Tom, Steak Supreme, Grey Poupon mustard, Regina wine vinegar and cooking wines, Ortega Mexican food, Chun King, Brer Rabbit molasses, College Inn chicken and beef products, My T Fine puddings, Vermont maid syrup, Davis baking powder	1925
Holland American Wafer Co.	Dutch Twin wafer cookie products P/L and generic wafer cookie products	1983
Husky Industries	Royal Oak and P/L charcoal and charcoal starter	1982
Keebler Co.	Ready-Crust pie crusts	1983
Keyes Fibre Company, Chinet Division	Chinet paper plates, napkins & plastic flatware	1974
Joan of Arc Company	Joan of Arc beans, fruit & vegetables, private label fruit and vegetables	1923
Lehn & Fink Products Company	Lysol products, Pine Action cleaner, Mop & Glo and Perk floor care products, Wet Ones moist towelettes	1964
Mauna Loa Macadamia Nut Company	Mauna Loa macadamia nut products	1974
Mc Ilhenny Company	Tabasco sauce and Bloody Mary mix	1926
Michigan Sugar Company	Pioneer sugar	1978
Ovaltine Products	Ovaltine hot chocolate, Fiddle Faddle, Yellow Screaming Zonkers	1983
Ragu Foods, Inc.	Ragu spaghetti sauces and cooking sauces, pizza quick sauces, crust mix and pizza kits, Adolph's meat tenderizers, marinades and salt substitutes	1979
Roman Household Products	Roman cleanser	1982
Sanna Division—Beatrice Foods Company	Swiss Miss cocoas and chocolate milk maker, Sanalac dry milk	1976
Seafare Foods Corp.	Seafare canned crabmeat, smoked salmon and sturgeon	1983
Shedd-Bartush Foods	Mario olives, Liberty cherries	1983
Southland Canning & Packing Co.	Orleans canned shrimp, oysters & clams	1983
Stinson Canning Company	Neptune sardines and canned fish specialties; Beach Cliff sardines and canned fish specialties	1926
Sun-Diamond Growers of California	Diamond walnut and pecan meats, Sunsweet prune juice	1929

(*continued*)

TABLE 3.3. (*Continued*)

Principal	Product lines	Date appointed
c. Grocery (continued)		
Sunnyland Refining Co., Inc.	Superman peanut butter	1982
Sunshine Feed Mills	Sunshine dry dog food	1975
Treesweet Products Company	Treesweet aseptic citrus juices	1934
John W. Taylor Packing Company	Taylor canned sweet potatoes and Irish potatoes; North American sauces	1924
Union Carbide Corp.	Glad plastic wrap & bags	1983
Vlasic Foods, Inc.	Vlasic pickles, relishes, peppers, sauerkraut, and specialty items	1979
Welch Foods, Inc.	Welch grape juices, jams, jellies, preserves and Welchade drinks	1978
Whitman's Chocolates	Whitman's chocolate morsels and baking chocolate	1983
Wicks Agriculture	Jack Rabbit dried beans, rice and popcorn	1933
Wilderness Foods—Div. Cherry Central	Wilderness fruit fillings, Wilderness apple juice and applesauce	1974
Wilson's Corn Products	Wilson's corn meal products and bird seed	1967
d. Health and beauty aids		
Abbott Laboratories	Selsun blue shampoos, Murine eye and ear drops, Lensine—clear eyes	1978
Ayerst Laboratories	Riopan antacid products	1981
Chesebrough-Ponds, Inc.	Vaseline intensive care lotion and bath, Beads & Dermatology formula lotion, Ponds creams and cleansing lotion, Rave permanents and hair sprays, Q-Tip cotton swabs, Vaseline petroleum jelly, Cutex nail polish removers and nail enamel	1980
Dep Corporation	Dep grooming products, pear soap	1980
Hawaiian Tropics	Hawaiian Tropics suntan products	1982
Lehn & Fink Products Company	Chubs–Tussy–Ogilvie products	1964
L'Oreal-Cosmair	Ultra Rich shampoos, Preference and Excellence haircolors	1981
McNeil Consumer Products	Tylenol and Co-Tylenol products	1981
Rexall Drug/Pro Corp.	Rexall vitamins, Pro brush toothbrushes	1980
Tampax, Inc.	Tampax tampons and maxithin pads	1981
Vidal Sassoon, Inc.	Vidal Sassoon shampoo, finishing rinse, hair spray and hair brushes	1982
White Labs	Soft Shave shaving lotion	1982
e. Perishable–frozen/produce–dairy/deli/meat		
Adolph's—Div. Ragu Foods, Inc.	Adolph's (meat dept.) meat marinades, meat loaf & beef stew mixes	1979
Arden, Inc.	Arden rice cakes	1983
Armour & Company	Armour frozen classic dinners	1983

TABLE 3.3. (Continued)

Principal	Product lines	Date appointed
e. *Perishable–frozen/produce–dairy/deli/meat* (continued)		
Beatrice Cheese Company	County Line natural cheeses	1977
Bordo Products Company	Bordo imported dates	1940
Brilliant Seafood, Inc.	Brilliant frozen shrimp	1980
Coca-Cola Company Foods Div.	Minute Maid frozen and chilled citrus juices and ades	1983
Chef Francisco	Oregon Farms frozen cakes, frozen crumb cakes and cupcakes	1979
Cole Bakeries, Inc.	Cole's frozen garlic breads, french bread, pizzas, birthday cakes and garlic spread	1982
Edwards Baking Company	Edwards frozen individual pie slices	1983
Elias Brothers Restaurants, Inc.	Big Boy refrigerated salad dressings	1983
Fisher Cheese Company	Fisher cheeses	1965
Green Giant Company	Green Giant frozen vegetables and entrees	1978
Jeno's Inc.	Jeno's frozen pizza, snacks & entrees	1974
Johnsonville Sausage, Inc.	Stayer's Johnsonville sausage products	1983
Kaukauna Cheese Div. International Multifoods	Kaukauna & P/L cheese spreads, cheese balls and logs	1983
King's Hawaiian Bread	King's Hawaiian bread & rolls	1981
Mrs. Paul's Kitchen, Inc.	Mrs. Paul's frozen fish, clams, chicken & vegetable products	1981
Newly Weds Foods, Inc.	Newly Weds refrigerated English muffins	1978
Old Orchard Brands, Inc.	Old Orchard frozen apple juices Four Seasons frozen fruit beverage	1983
Paradise Fruit Company, Inc.	Paradise glazed fruit	1965
Rich Products Corp.	Rich's frozen bread doughs, pies, eclairs, short cakes and Coffee Rich	1983
Ruiz Food Products, Inc.	Rosita-Si! Frozen Mexican entrees	1983
Sanna Division—Beatrice Foods Company	Swiss Miss refrigerated puddings and frozen pudding bars	1976
Seaboard Seed Co.	Song & Beauty bird food, grass seed	1982
Snow King Frozen Foods, Inc.	Snow King frozen sandwich steaks	1983
Sun-Diamond Growers of California	Diamond in-shell walnuts and mixed nuts, Sunsweet prunes and dried fruit, Sun-Maid Raisins, nature snacks, and cut fruit, Blue Ribbon figs, Holiday in-shell nuts	1929
Superior Seafoods, Inc.	Captain fresh fish & seafood	1981
Treesweet Products Company	Treesweet frozen citrus juices	1934
Universal Foods Corporation	Red Star Yeasts, Stella cheeses	1979
Vlasic Foods, Inc.	Vlasic (deli) dills	1979
Welch Foods, Inc.	Welch chilled juice drinks, Welch frozen grape and cranberry juices, Welchade frozen drinks	1978

Michigan State University	REQUEST FOR QUOTATION

DATE: JUNE 10, 1987

NO. 1954

PLEASE NOTE THIS IS NOT AN ORDER

ADDRESS REPLY TO:
MICHIGAN STATE UNIVERSITY
PURCHASING DEPARTMENT
PURCHASING BUILDING
EAST LANSING, MICH. 48824

1.
2.
E. Reneaud Corp
207 Alaskan Highway
Blank City, USA

INSTRUCTIONS FOR BIDDERS

1. Submit quotations on this form only.
2. If substitutes are offered attach or write on this form full specifications.
3. If a better price can be offered by slightly changing quantities requested please advise and quote on that amount.
4. Unless otherwise stated, there is no restriction on the quantities that may be ordered, either more or less.
5. All prices will be considered F.O.B. destination unless otherwise indicated. If prices are quoted F.O.B. shipping point, please indicate total transportation charges.
6. Unless otherwise noted by the vendor, prices quoted are firm and this bid will be considered open for a period of 45 days from due date noted.
7. This inquiry implies no obligation on the part of the buyer. This is not an order.
8. In case of default by vendor, M.S.U. Purchasing Department may procure the articles or services from other sources and hold the vendor responsible for any excess cost occasioned thereby which includes loss of research time.

QUOTATION DUE BY: August 14, 1987

NOTE

RETURN TO ATTENTION: D. Ziolkowski

FOR QUESTIONS RE BID
PH. 517-353-2977

ITEM	QUANTITY	UNIT	DESCRIPTION	NET UNIT PRICE	TOTAL AMOUNT
1.	150	cs.	Peaches Diced - Yellow Cling - U.S. Choice Light Syrup 6/10	$14.00	$ 2,100
2.	800	cs	Peaches - Sliced - Yellow Cling - U.S. Choice Light Syrup 6/10	$13.50	$10,800
3.	400	cs.	Fruit Cocktail - U.S. Choice Light Syrup 6/10	$15.25	$ 6,100

BUYERS C & O SIDING   ALL PRODUCTS 1987 PACK

MAIL IN ENCLOSED WHITE ENVELOPE

DELIVERY WEEK OF SEPTEMBER 28, 1987......

VENDOR ID NO.	CHECK IF APPLICABLE	☐ MINORITY BUS. ☐ SMALL BUS.	TOTAL	$19,000.

PRICES F.O.B.
FOOD STORES

SHIPMENT PROMISE AFTER RECEIPT OF ORDER   20   DAYS

SUGGEST BEST WAY TO SHIP   RAIL

TERMS
NET 30

YOUR QUOTATION NO
#3304

QUOTED BY (SIGNATURE)
Gladys Guest

DATE
8 /05 /87

NOTICE TO ALL SUPPLIERS: On April 18, 1969 the Board of Trustees of Michigan State University adopted a policy of requiring proof of equal employment practices from all University suppliers. Effective November 19, 1969 the following non-discrimination clause is hereby incorporated into and made a part of all request for quotations and purchase orders issued by Michigan State University:
   The supplier in bidding and/or filling a purchase order agrees not to discriminate against any employee or applicant for employment, with respect to hire, tenure, terms, conditions or privileges of employment, or any matter directly or indirectly related to employment, because of race, color, religion, national origin or ancestry. The supplier further agrees that every subcontractor or order given for the supplying of this order will contain a provision requiring non-discrimination in employment, as herein specified. This covenant is required pursuant to Section 4 of Act No. 251, Public Acts of the State of Michigan of 1955 as amended and any breach thereof may be regarded as a material breach of the contract or purchase order.

MSU is an Affirmative Action/Equal Opportunity Institution

FIG. 3.4.   Completed request for quotation with vendor's bid stating prices and terms offered.

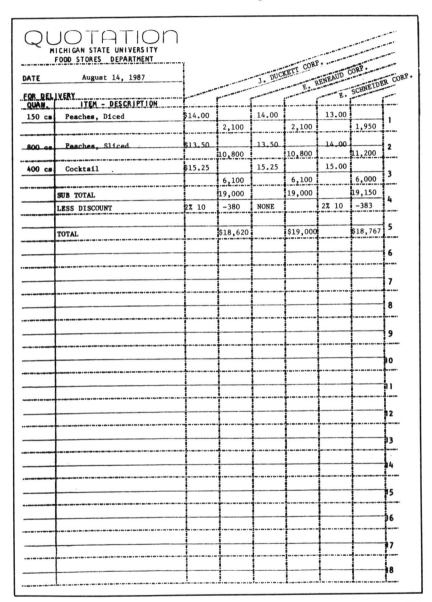

FIG. 3.5.   An evaluation sheet makes it easier to compare bids from different vendors. This is especially helpful when a large number of bids have been received.

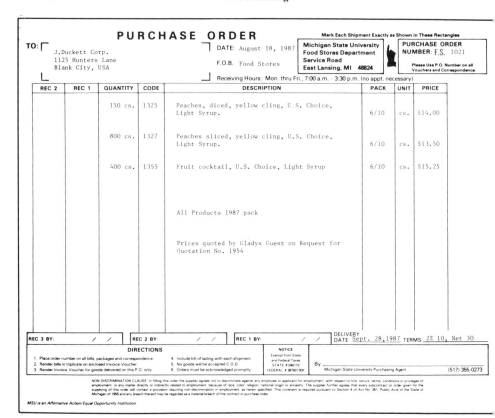

FIG. 3.6.   A purchase order is issued to the company that submits the lowest bid.

request a *quotation*, or bid, from companies wishing to supply these items. Everything else being equal, a school would accept the bid and purchase the goods from the company offering the lowest quote.

A *request for quotation* informs potential vendors what items are needed and in what quantity, when the product and the quotation is due and whom to contact if they have questions. Preprinted forms often are used to standardize and facilitate the preparation of requests. Figure 3.3 (p.53) shows a completed form with a request for canned peaches.

Let us suppose that this request for peaches is sent to three companies: E. Reneaud Corp., J. Duckett Corp. and E. Schneider Corp. The quotation returned by the E. Reneaud Corp is shown in Fig. 3.4. The vendor has filled in not only the prices it is offering but also the terms (in this case, no discount is offered), the promised shipment date, and suggested mode of transportation. Note that item 5 in the instructions for bidders specifies F.O.B. destination unless the bidder indicates otherwise.

Michigan State University
Food Stores Building
Service Road
East Lansing, MI 48824

May 18, 1987

Number of locations placing orders and receiving deliveries: 20 Cafeterias, and 14 Snack Shops

Contract Starting Date: July 1, 1987

Contract Expiration Date: June 30, 1988

Invitation, Bid and Acceptance of Potato Chips and Related Products as listed below:

Sealed bids in duplicate will be received by the Manager of Food Stores, Michigan State University, Service Road, East Lansing, MI 48824 until 3:30 P.M. Thursday, June 18, 1987. Bids will be opened at that time.

Description		Price ($)/ pound (lb)	Anticipated usage (lb)	Total cost to M.S.U. ($)
Item	Size			
1. Potato Chips—Regular	Bulk	1.00	3000	3,000
2. Potato Chips—Wavy	Bulk	1.00	40000	40,000
3. Potato Chips—Flavor*	Bulk	1.30	5000	6,500
4. Corn Chips	Bulk	0.85	10000	8,500
5. Pretzel Twists	Bulk	0.75	4000	3,000
6. Cheese Twists	Bulk	0.88	4000	3,520
7. Popcorn—Regular	Bulk	1.00	150	150
8. Popcorn—Cheese	Bulk	1.30	500	650
9. Nacho Chips	Bulk	.88	7500	6,600

Items 10–21 (resale items) must be in unpriced packages

		Price ($)/ ounce (oz)	(oz)	($)
10. Potato Chips—Regular	Vending	0.111	40,000	4,440
11. Potato Chips—Regular	Medium	0.091	2,000	182
12. Potato Chips—Wavy	Vending	0.111	40,000	4,440
13. Potato Chips—Wavy	Medium	0.091	1,000	91
14. Potato Chips—Flavor*	Vending	0.130	50,000	6,500
15. Potato Chips—Flavor*	Medium	0.111	3,500	3,885
16. Nacho Chips	Vending	0.130	2,500	325
17. Corn Chips	Vending	0.062	8,000	496
18. Popcorn—Cheese	Vending	0.135	20,000	2,700
19. Popcorn—Cheese	Medium	0.140	1,000	140
20. Cheese Twists	Vending	0.122	6,000	732
21. Pretzel Twists	Vending	0.111	10,000	1,110
			Grand total	$96,961

*Flavor chips are a combination of B.B.Q., green onion and sour cream.

FIG. 3.7.   Completed bid form submitted by vendor for an annual contract for potato chips. This is just part of a lengthy document stating the terms and specifications of the contract, which a vendor must agree to fulfill as part of its bid.

Michigan State University
Food Stores Department

Potato Chip Contract
1987–1988

Bids must be submitted on this form and in accordance with all conditions listed hereon. Bids and amendments thereto, or withdrawals of bids must be received in writing by the Manager of Food Stores, Michigan State University, prior to the date and time specified for the public bid opening: 3:30 P.M., Thursday, June 18, 1987.

"Michigan State University," as applied in this contract, shall hereafter be referred to as "MSU."

Bids shall be submitted in a sealed envelope, addressed to: Manager, Food Stores, Michigan State University, Service Road, East Lansing, Michigan 48824. Clearly mark *Potato Chip Bid* with the name of the bidder on the back of the envelope. Each vendor is responsible for bid delivery to Food Stores. MSU cannot be held responsible for any bid received after the bid opening. No oral modifications will be considered. Bids received after 3:30 P.M., Thursday, June 18, 1987, will not be considered, and will be returned to the bidder unopened.

The Manager of MSU Food Stores reserves the right to reject any or all bids, or to accept any bid which, in the opinion of MSU officials, will better serve the University.

One total contract shall be awarded to one supplier for the period specified. The contract shall be awarded to the supplier meeting all 23 general conditions and offering the lowest "Grand Total" cost to MSU.

General Conditions

1. Effective Date of This Contract: July 1, 1987 for a period of one (1) year, expiring on June 30, 1988. This contract may be extended for one (1) year.
2. Attach a letter outlining, by section, any condition your firm cannot meet and your alternate proposal for that condition.
3. The Manager of MSU Food Stores will be the administrator and the supplier's contact for the duration of this contract. The supplier must assign a management staff member as the contact for MSU. This staff member will be responsible for regular inspections and reports to the Manager of MSU Food Stores for all phases of this contract.
4. The supplier receiving the bid must be an equal opportunity employer. Failure to comply during the life of the contract will be grounds for cancellation.
5. Each supplier must bid on, and be able to supply, all products outlined in this contract.
6. This contract or any parts thereof cannot be assigned, transferred or subcontracted to another company, or individual, without full written consent and approval of the Manager of MSU Food Stores.
7. The supplier guarantees to protect MSU, its agents or employees from liability of any nature or kind in connection with their contract by either acts or omissions. The supplier must furnish adequate protection from damages to MSU property and must repair damages of any kind for which the vendor, its suppliers, or its employees are responsible. The suppliers or their employees are responsible.
8. The supplier must carry the following minimum insurance with companies authorized to do business in Michigan and acceptable to MSU:

A.	Workers' Compensation	Statutory
	Employer's Liability	$100,000
B.	Comprehensive General Liability	
	1. Bodily Injury	Each occurrence
	2. Property Damage	Each occurrence
C.	Comprehensive Automotive Liability	
	1. Bodily Injury	Each person
		Each occurrence
	2. Property Damage	Each occurrence
D.	Umbrella Liability	
	Bodily Injury and Property Damage combined	Each occurrence

Note: Any combination of primary and umbrella limits in B, C, and D above total $500,000 in each category.

The supplier awarded the contract must name MSU as an "Additional Insured" in the Public Liability Insurance policy. Copies of all policies must be submitted to MSU Food Stores at least eight (8) days prior to the commencement of the contract.
This insurance must remain in force for the duration of the contract.

9. Any designee, either an employee or authorized representative of MSU, may, unannounced, accompany the supplier's employees on their campus rounds. The supplier agrees that all warehouses, manufacturing plants, etc., servicing MSU shall be subject to inspection by any person designated by MSU at any reasonable times.

10. If a labor dispute between the vendor and its employees, or a union results in the picketing of, or a work stoppage by, any MSU employee, MSU may immediately cancel this contract.

11. Either party to this agreement may cancel this contract by giving no less than sixty (60) days written notice to the other party. If the contract is cancelled it must be at the end of a school term.

12. Bidders are invited and urged to inspect the thirty-four (34) delivery locations prior to submitting bids. Over the period of the contract some units may either be added or deleted. Delivery is to the storerooms of the twenty-four (24) locations.

13. Prices and calculations must be stated in units of items specified. Attach a letter indicating your size and pack for each item listed. Flavor chips are to include B.B.Q., Green Onion and Sour Cream. Vending size is approximately 1 oz and medium 8 oz. (Each company will probably be a little different.)

14. Deliveries are to be made to the campus three days per week (Monday, Tuesday and Friday). Units West of Farm Lane shall be served on Monday and units East of Farm Lane on Tuesday. A Friday delivery shall be made to Brody, Crossroads, Kellogg Center, Union and any other unit that requests a delivery. Any unit may place a special order on Thursday (by 4:30 P.M.) for delivery on Friday. Deliveries are not required on the University's recognized holidays.

15. Between terms and summer delivery schedules will be reduced to one (1) day per week. Schedule to be set up with MSU.

16. Bids must be on suppliers first grade only. Samples will be required from the low bidder prior to receiving the contract award. All items must meet or surpass Federal and State regulations. During the contract, customer complaints may necessitate MSU to require a change in product or brand by the supplier.

17. One blanket purchase order will be issued by MSU. The invoicing must be done on MSU Voucher Forms and submitted to MSU Food Stores on either a monthly or bi-monthly basis.

18. The supplier must furnish a numbered delivery ticket (2 copies) for each delivery and signed for in each food unit. No signature—no payment. One copy of each delivery ticket must be left with the merchandise in each food unit; the second copy to be submitted to MSU Food Stores by the supplier at the beginning of the next week's delivery.

19. The supplier awarded the contract may be asked to supply other standard merchandise, or procure items from other suppliers. Approval of items and prices must first be obtained from the Manager of MSU Food Stores before being placed on the approved list. Attach a letter listing other standard merchandise available and your prices for each.

20. If ingredient or packaging costs substantially increase or decrease, the supplier or MSU may request a conference to discuss those items affected.

21. This contract does not include products for vending machines.

22. At the conclusion of the year's contract the supplier will furnish MSU with an itemized report, per item, of the total volume supplied MSU for the period July 1 through June 30. This report is due by August 29 (60 days). Format must be approved by MSU.

23. This agreement constitutes the entire contract between the parties with respect to the matters covered herein and there are no oral understandings or agreements with respect thereto. No variation or modification of this agreement and no waiver of its provisions shall be valid unless it is in writing and signed by the duly authorized officers of the vendor and MSU.

Date _____

Firm name: _____
By (signed): _____
By (print): _____
Title: _____
Address: _____

In compliance with the invitation for bids and subject to all 23 General Conditions listed, the undersigned offers and agrees to deliver all of the items for which prices are quoted, at the price set opposite each item for the total length of this contract. [See Fig. 3.7.]

Date _____

Firm name: _____
By (signed): _____
By (print): _____
Title: _____
Address: _____

. . . .

Acceptance by Michigan State University: The acceptance of the items indicated above constitutes a contract between Michigan State University and the Supplier whose name appears above.

Date accepted: _____ Title _____

_____
Michigan State University

FIG. 3.8. Complete potato chip contract.

FIG. 3.9.   Annual contracts for commodities (e.g., egg, butter, meat) whose prices fluctuate can be based on current market prices.

In this example, with three companies being asked to submit bids, it would not be too difficult to determine the best offer by just reading each quote. However, in order to avoid errors, especially when five to ten suppliers are quoting, it is best to write out the bids on a spread sheet like that in Fig. 3.5. The Duckett and Reneaud companies quoted identical prices for all three products, but Duckett offered a cash discount so its total bid was less. E. Schneider Corp. quoted the lowest price on two items, but its quote for the big-volume item (sliced peaches) was $.50 more per case than the quotes of the other two companies. By offering the 2% 10 discount, E. Schneider Corp. moved into second place. Based on these quotations, the director of purchasing would issue a *purchase order* to J. Duckett Corporation (Fig. 3.6).

Another type of request for quotation commonly used by foodservice operations is for goods that are to be delivered throughout the school year. In this case, schools take bids, usually in the spring, for products and services for the next school year. Typical products that are purchased on annual contracts are bread, dairy products, snack items (potato chips, pretzels) and soft drinks.

The usual procedure in requesting quotations for annual contracts is to send a cover letter explaining the bid procedure to qualified vendors capable of fulfilling the bid specifications. Attached to the letter are three copies of the specifications and bid form. The specifications are very detailed and describe all the responsibilities of the vendor. When a bid is accepted by the school and the specifications are signed by the vendor, this document becomes the *legal contract* between them. Figure 3.7 shows the completed bid form returned by one company in response to a request by Michigan State University for an annual contract for potato chips. The complete contract is shown in Fig. 3.8.

Annual contracts for butter, eggs, meat or any commodity whose price is not constant during the life of the contract generally are based on the current market price. Figure 3.9 shows a request for quotation on fresh eggs, ordered and delivered on a weekly basis. Each bidder is instructed to base its delivered price on "Urner Barry's Price Current," a weekly market report. A quote might be $\frac{3}{4}$¢, $\frac{1}{4}$¢ or any amount over the market price on a given day. In a very competitive situation the quotation might be $\frac{1}{8}$¢ *under* the specified market price.

REFERENCES

AGRI-COMMODITIES. 1983. Meat Price Relationships. Agri-Commodities, Inc., North Andover, MA.

ANON. 1978. Know how to read the food labels. Changing Times 2, 36.

U.S. DEPT. OF HEALTH AND HUMAN SERVICES. Read the Label, Set a Better Table. Pub. no. 76–2049. Food and Drug Administration, Washington, DC.

U.S. DEPT. OF HEALTH AND HUMAN SERVICES. 1974. Nutrition Labelling Terms You Should Know. Pub. no. 74–2010. Food and Drug Administration, Washington, DC.

FEDERAL REGISTER. 1975. Canned fruit standards. 4(27), 5762–5765.

FONTANA, B. and ORDELL, G. 1983. A New Food Center for University of Virginia. NACAS, April 1983.

KOTSCHEVAR, L. H. 1975. Quantity Food Purchasing. John Wiley & Sons, New York, NY.

NATIONAL ASSOCIATION OF MEAT PURVEYORS. 1978. Meat Buyers Guide. National Association of Meat Purveyors, Tuscon, AZ.

PEDDERSEN, R. B. 1977. SPECS, The Comprehensive Foodservice Purchasing & Specification Manual. Cahners Books Internationa, Boston, MA.

SACHAROW, S. 1979. Packaging Regulations. AVI Publishing Co., Westport, CT.

THOMAS PUBLISHING CO. 1983. Thomas Grocery Register. Thomas Publishing Co., New York, NY.

THORNER, M. E. and MANNING, P. D. 1983. Quality Control in Foodservice. Revised Edition. AVI Publishing Co., Westport, CT.

 Budgeting

A good budget not only tells the foodservice manager where he or she has been, but also helps in planning the path for the future. This is especially important in today's computerized society. The systematic process of using a budget not only allows the manager to estimate income and expenses, but allows for periodic review and adjustment as the year progresses. Food cost reports are invaluable in setting up a budget. Precosting is an important step in the periodic adjustments that need to be made.

HISTORICAL FINANCIAL RECORDS

The first step in developing any budget is to gather financial information about how an organization has operated in the past. All schools probably have this information available. Unfortunately, it is not always broken down into components useful for budgeting.

For example, a manager knowing only the foodservice's total income and total expenses for the previous school year, cannot set up a meaningful budget for next year. In such a situation, when data are not available in useful categories, it may take 2 years to get a budget system working. During the first year, data would be collected that could be useful in preparing a budget for the second year.

The income from previous years should be available. The number of customers and the income per week, month and quarter or semester should all be available. This historical data will be used in estimating the income for the coming year in the budget planning.

MSU Department of Residence Halls
ESTIMATED AND ACTUAL
REVENUES AND EXPENSES

_____ HALL   Cafeteria ☐   School Year _____
Snackshop ☐

MONTH →										TOTALS
INCOME	Est									
	Actual									
To Date	Est									
	Actual									
PERSONAL SERVICES	Est									
	Actual									
To Date	Est									
	Actual									
FRINGE BENEFITS	Est									
	Actual									
To Date	Est									
	Actual									
FOOD SUPPLIES	Est									
	Actual									
To Date	Est									
	Actual									
RESALE ITEMS	Est									
	Actual									
To Date	Est									
	Actual									
LAUNDRY & CLEANING	Est									
	Actual									
To Date	Est									
	Actual									
GENERAL EXPENSES	Est									
	Actual									
To Date	Est									
	Actual									
PROGRAMING SERVICES	Est									
	Actual									
To Date	Est									
	Actual									
UTILITY SERVICES	Est									
	Actual									
To Date	Est									
	Actual									
EQUIPMENT	Est									
	Actual									
To Date	Est									
	Actual									
SUPPLIES & MATERIALS	Est									
	Actual									
To Date	Est									
	Actual									
REPAIR & MAINTENANCE	Est									
	Actual									
To Date	Est									
	Actual									
TOTAL MONTHLY EXPENSE	Est									
	Actual									
To Date	Est									
	Actual									
NET MONTHLY INCOME	Est									
	Actual									
YEAR TO DATE	Est									
	Actual									

FIG. 4.1.   Complete budget form, including spaces for income and all expense categories plus estimated, actual, monthly and year-to-date figures.

Expenses incurred by a foodservice operation in previous years should also be available for the manager. Although the divisions may not be detailed in the most useful form, the total figures can be used. For example, a report may list expenses in only three categories: food, non-food items and labor. The new budget will probably contain more items but they could be lumped into these three categories. The expense categories listed in Fig. 4.1 could be grouped into these three categories: (1) labor—includes personal services and fringe benefits, (2) food—includes food supplies and resale items and (3) non-food items—includes all other items. In this manner a starting place for proposed expenses could begin.

Once the necessary data is at hand, a manager can begin to estimate expenses and revenues for the period to be covered by the budget. If the projected income is less than the projected expenses, some adjustments may be needed so that the foodservice operation does not incur a loss.

ESTIMATING EXPENSES

The foodservice manager should divide the expenses into meaningful categories. Those used in the Michigan State operation are listed in Fig. 4.1. Then comes the difficult task of estimating the new year's expenses. By reviewing last year's expenditures, an estimate is made depending on whether the usage is expected to be the same, higher or lower. Combine that information with this year's prices to estimate projected expenses.

A few telephone calls to those people supplying goods and services will help to identify where there will be increased costs of operation. As an example, the telephone company (categorized under Utility Services) has an 8% increase scheduled for January 1. Because this date occurs halfway through the school year it is easy to calculate the increase. Based on the same usage as last year, the budget would show no increase for the first 6 months. The last 6 months would be calculated at 108%.

The basic rate for the phones in the operation is $80 per month. In addition, last year long-distance calls fluctuated between $13 and $28 with an average of $20 per month. We have budgeted $100 ($80 basic + $20 long distance) per month for the first 6 months, and $106 ($80 basic + 8% + $20 long distance) per month for the last 6 months, giving us a total budget of $1,238 for the year.

It will be necessary to go through the expenses in each category on a monthly basis and calculate the anticipated costs. It is important to keep in mind several changes that may occur in the new year.

Some Things to Anticipate

1. Is the same customer count expected next year? How will that affect each cost category?
2. Will the school sessions be during the same weeks next year? Starting school a week earlier or later will throw costs off for that month.
3. Will there be the same number of paydays next December as there were the year before? If the staff is paid every 2 weeks you will have some months with three paydays.
4. When are pay increases due for employees? How much, and in what month do they take effect?
5. Is someone retiring next year? Will that person be replaced, and if so, when? Will a lump sum be paid to the retiree for sick leave accumulations? Will the new person get the same salary or will it be less?
6. Is some equipment in need of repair or replacement?
7. Are any of the fringe benefits going to increase? (For example, is the contract for health expiring in March; a dental plan starting on January 1; the Social Security percentage increasing on January 1?)
8. Was there a major renovation last year (e.g., the kitchen floor being replaced), which would cause this year's maintenance budget to be less?

By adding all of the anticipated expenses, income needs for the new year can be calculated.

ESTIMATING INCOME

If projected sales for the new year are equal to the sales of the past year, these income figures may be used in preparing the new budget. If the anticipated income is greater than budgeted expenses there is no need to increase prices.

Most years it will not be that easy. If expenses are greater than income, it will be necessary to (1) increase income, (2) decrease expenses, or (3) do a combination of the two.

Using an example of budgeted expenses exceeding anticipated income by $10,000, the three choices would result in (1) raising income by $10,000, (2) reducing expenditures by $10,000, or (3) increasing income by $4,000 and decreasing expenses by $6,000. Any other combination could be used to achieve the $10,000 figure.

The easiest way to increase income is to charge an across-the-board percentage increase. If the budget is $10,000 short and last year's income was $100,000, a 10% increase on all items is needed.

Two basic methods are used when increasing prices on a la carte menu items.

These are (1) a straight across-the-board percentage increase on each item, and (2) an increase in certain items in a given category. Each item within the category is considered separately. With both methods, prices are rounded off.

The straight across-the-board method is usually used when the menu is limited. This method causes some problems. If a 2% increase is used, any item under $1.15 would not increase in price, items from $1.15 to $3.75 would increase by a nickel.

Most operations increase prices by category because increases in food costs normally fluctuate by category. Beef items are affected as a group, as are pork, dairy, etc. If it is decided that 10% more income is needed and that price increases will be made, it is time to look at historical records. How many of what items were sold? How much extra income would be derived by increasing the price of milk $0.05? How much would be derived by charging $0.10 more for a hot dog, hamburger or New York strip steak?

Let us go back to the example where $10,000 additional income is needed. If 200,000 hamburgers are sold per year, it may be decided to increase tbe price of hamburger by $0.05 and leave the remaining prices as they are. An example of price increasing by category to obtain an additional $10,000 is shown in Table 4.1.

One fallacy with this method of price increasing is the assumption that the quantities sold in each category will remain constant. As an extreme example, what happens when we increase only one item to get the needed $10,000? The records show that 1,000 rib eye steaks were sold last year at $3 each. That means an increase of $10 per steak is needed to get the $10,000 added income. The new menu price would be $13. We not only would not get the proposed $10,000 added income, but we would price ourselves out of the market and probably would not sell any rib eye steaks. If no sales occur the income would go down by $3,000 ($3 × 1,000).

Profits or Excess

The use of the word profit or excess in an operation that is supposed to be a nonprofit organization can be a problem. A college foodservice that grosses a million dollars a year and has expenses of $10,000 less than that, has made a profit of $10,000. As soon as the financial report is published, the student newspaper may print an article indicating that the foodservice operation made a profit off of the students last year. Bad public relations results. In the true sense of the word, there really is no profit.

Most schools publish financial reports. In these reports the terms profit or excess are often no longer used. The managers are not trying to hide anything—they just want the budget to reflect the true use of the funds. In many instances a manager may be trying to build up funds over a period of years to pay for repairs,

TABLE 4.1.   Price Increase by Category

Category	Item	Quantity sold last yr (ea)	Proposed increase (¢)	Increased income ($)	Total increase ($)
Beef:	Hamburgers	80,000	5	$4,000	
	Rib eye steaks	1,000	10	100	
	Beef stew	10,000	5	500	
	Beef burgundy	2,000	10	200	
	Beef loaf	5,000	5	250	
	Beef pot roast	10,000	5	500	
	Beef burritos	10,000	10	1,000	
	Beef ravioli	10,000	5	500	
					7,050
Cheese and egg:	Cheese sandwich	10,000	0		
	Cheese souffle	20,000	0		
	Egg foo young	10,000	0		
	Egg a la king	5,000	5	250	
	Eggwich–bun	5,000	0		
	Nachos–cheese	6,000	5	300	
					550
Fish:	Baked cod	10,000	0		
	Baked sole	10,000	0		
	Fried clams	20,000	0		
	Fish stick–bun	10,000	0		
	Fried catfish	8,000	0		
	Seafood crepes	9,000	0		
	Seafood newburg	1,000	0		
	Shrimp creole	1,000	0		
	Tuna noodle casserole	6,000	0		
					0
Poultry:	Chix a la king	10,000	5	500	
	Baked chix	8,000	5	400	
	BBQ chix	5,000	5	250	
	Chix patty–bun	6,000	5	300	
	Chix salad boat	4,000	5	200	
	Turkey noodle bake	3,000	5	150	
	Turkey sandwich	6,000	5	300	
	Turkey souffle	10,000	5	500	
					2,600
Pork and ham:	B.L.T. sandwich	4,000	0		
	BBQ pork–bun	8,000	0		
	BBQ ribs	60,000	0		
	Hot dog–bun	5,000	0		
	Baked ham	10,000	0		
	Ham sandwich–bun	8,000	0		
	Monte Cristo sandwich	4,000	0		
					0
				Total	$10,200

remodeling or new equipment. If the words excess or profit are used in a financial report, misunderstandings may result.

Budget lines labeled "money available for major repairs," "money available for debt service," "money available to lower cost of room and board," or any words that show the true meaning of what the excess money is for would be appropriate.

A budget does the following for a manager:

1. Estimates expenses
2. Determines income needed to cover those expenses
3. Allows for periodic reviews of both income and expenses and allows the manager to make intelligent adjustments

SAMPLE BUDGET

Assume that you are in charge of Underwood Hall Cafeteria, which is a 500-student residence hall on the campus of a large university. The budget form being used for Underwood Hall Cafeteria is shown in Fig. 4.2.

The school has already determined that each student will pay $6 per day for

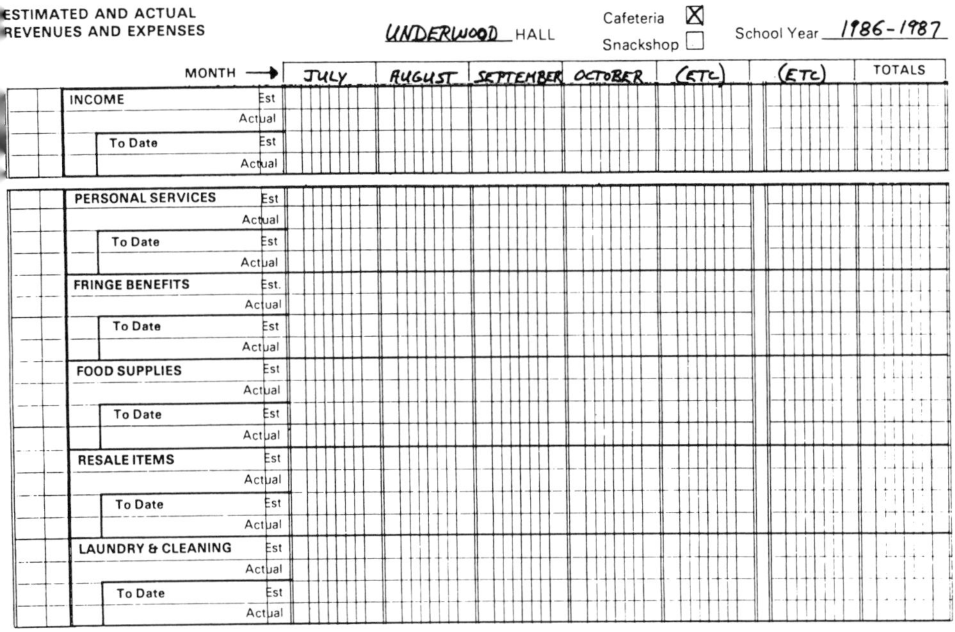

FIG. 4.2. Initial portion of Underwood Hall's budget sheet.

MSU Department of Residence Halls
ESTIMATED AND ACTUAL
REVENUES AND EXPENSES   _UNDERWOOD_ HALL   Cafeteria ☒   School Year _1986-1987_
                                                                 Snackshop ☐

MONTH →	JULY	AUGUST	SEPTEMBER	OCTOBER	(ETC)	(ETC)	TOTALS
INCOME	Est	0	21000	90000	93000			
	Actual							
To Date	Est							
	Actual							
PERSONAL SERVICES	Est							
	Actual							
To Date	Est							
	Actual							
FRINGE BENEFITS	Est							
	Actual							
To Date	Est							
	Actual							
FOOD SUPPLIES	Est							
	Actual							
To Date	Est							
	Actual							
RESALE ITEMS	Est							
	Actual							
To Date	Est							
	Actual							
LAUNDRY & CLEANING	Est							
	Actual							
To Date	Est							
	Actual							

FIG. 4.3.   Budget form containing estimated income.

board. The hall will be closed for painting of students' rooms in July so that it will be ready for the opening of scbool on August 25.

Estimated Gross Income

Estimated income is calculated as follows and inserted on the budget sheet (Fig. 4.3).

July	Closed for painting	$0
August	500 × $6 × 7 days =	$21,000
September	500 × $6 × 30 days =	$90,000
October	500 × $6 × 31 days =	$93,000

To-date calculations are obtained by adding income from the new month to the running total. Figure 4.4 now includes to-date income.

July		$0
August	Running total + $21,000 =	$21,000
September	Running total + $90,000 =	$111,000
October	Running total + $93,000 =	$204,000

Estimated Expenses

Payroll for full-time regular employees is $600 per day when school is not in session and the crew is scheduled Monday through Friday. During school the same amount of regulars are needed, but they are spread out over seven days. That means the regular payroll is $429 per day during the 7-day work weeks. Students are used only when school is in session. The anticipated payroll for student labor is $200 per day. Personal services (labor costs) both month and to-date are calculated below and listed in Fig. 4.5.

			Month	To-date
July	23 work days	× $600 (regular) =	$13,800	$13,800
August	16 preschool days	× $600 (regular) =	$9,600	
	7 school days	× $429 (regular) =	$3,003	
	7 school days	× $200 (student) =	$1,400	
			$14,003	$27,803
September	30 school days	× $429 (regular) =	$12,870	
	30 school days	× $200 (student) =	$6,000	
			$18,870	$46,673
October	31 school days	× $429 (regular) =	$13,299	
	31 school days	× $200 (student) =	$6,200	
			$19,499	$66,172

FIG. 4.4. Budget form containing estimated to-date income.

MSU Department of Residence Halls
ESTIMATED AND ACTUAL
REVENUES AND EXPENSES

UNDERWOOD HALL Cafeteria ☒ Snackshop ☐ School Year *1986-1987*

MONTH →		JULY	AUGUST	SEPTEMBER	OCTOBER	(ETC)	(ETC)	TOTALS
INCOME	Est	0	21000	90000	93000			
	Actual							
To Date	Est	0	21000	111000	204000			
	Actual							
PERSONAL SERVICES	Est	13800	14003	18870	19499			
	Actual							
To Date	Est	13800	27803	46673	66172			
	Actual							
FRINGE BENEFITS	Est.							
	Actual							
To Date	Est							
	Actual							
FOOD SUPPLIES	Est							
	Actual							
To Date	Est							
	Actual							
RESALE ITEMS	Est							
	Actual							
To Date	Est							
	Actual							
LAUNDRY & CLEANING	Est							
	Actual							
To Date	Est							
	Actual							

FIG. 4.5. Budget form including estimated personnel services expenses.

MSU Department of Residence Halls
ESTIMATED AND ACTUAL
REVENUES AND EXPENSES

UNDERWOOD HALL Cafeteria ☒ Snackshop ☐ School Year *1986-1987*

MONTH →		JULY	AUGUST	SEPTEMBER	OCTOBER	(ETC)	(ETC)	TOTALS
INCOME	Est	0	21000	90000	93000			
	Actual							
To Date	Est	0	21000	111000	204000			
	Actual							
PERSONAL SERVICES	Est	13800	14003	18870	19499			
	Actual							
To Date	Est	13800	27803	46673	66172			
	Actual							
FRINGE BENEFITS	Est.	3450	3457	3218	3325			
	Actual							
To Date	Est	3450	6601	9819	13144			
	Actual							
FOOD SUPPLIES	Est							
	Actual							
To Date	Est							
	Actual							
RESALE ITEMS	Est							
	Actual							
To Date	Est							
	Actual							
LAUNDRY & CLEANING	Est							
	Actual							
To Date	Est							
	Actual							

FIG. 4.6. Budget form including estimated fringe benefits expenses.

The next category in the budget is fringe benefits. In this example, fringe benefits are retirement costs, health care insurances and worker's compensation insurance. Regular employees are covered, but student employees are not. The personnel office has determined that the cafeteria will be charged a 25% overhead on the regular employees payroll. This overhead percentage pays for the fringe benefits and the calculated amounts are given in Fig. 4.6.

Food supplies is the next category. An amount of 36% of the monthly income is used to estimate food costs for that month ($2100 × 0.36 = $7560). Figure 4.7 now contains these estimated costs. For this example, only three expenses, personal services, fringe benefits and food supplies, are listed. Adding up these three expenses for 2 months we arrive at the total expenses for both the month and to-date.

		Month	To-date
July	Personal services	$13,800	
	Fringe benefits	3,450	
	Food supplies	0	
		$17,250	
			$17,250
August	Personal services	$14,003	
	Fringe benefits	3,151	
	Food supplies	7,560	
		$24,714	
			$41,964

MSU Department of Residence Halls
ESTIMATED AND ACTUAL
REVENUES AND EXPENSES   _UNDERWOOD_ HALL   Cafeteria ☒   Snackshop ☐   School Year _1986-1987_

MONTH →		JULY	AUGUST	SEPTEMBER	OCTOBER	(ETC)	(ETC)	TOTALS
INCOME	Est	0	21000	90000	93000			
	Actual							
To Date	Est	0	21000	111000	204000			
	Actual							
PERSONAL SERVICES	Est	13800	14003	18870	18499			
	Actual							
To Date	Est	13800	27803	46673	65172			
	Actual							
FRINGE BENEFITS	Est.	3450	3151	3218	3325			
	Actual							
To Date	Est	3450	6601	9819	13144			
	Actual							
FOOD SUPPLIES	Est	0	7560	32400	33480			
	Actual							
To Date	Est	0	7560	39960	73440			
	Actual							
RESALE ITEMS	Est							
	Actual							
To Date	Est							
	Actual							
LAUNDRY & CLEANING	Est							
	Actual							
To Date	Est							
	Actual							

FIG. 4.7. Budget form including estimated food supplies expenses.

FIG. 4.8.   Lower portion of budget form containing estimated total monthly expenses.

Looking at the bottom of the budget sheet, skipping the other expenses, find the total monthly expenses section displayed in Fig. 4.8. The total expenses for this example are listed on this budget form.

Estimated Net Income

By subtracting the estimated total monthly expenses from the estimated income at the top of the budget sheet (Fig. 4.7), estimated net monthly income is derived.

	Month	To-date
July income	$0	
Expenses	$17,250	
Net monthly income	−$17,250	−$17,250
August income	$21,000	
Expenses	24,714	
Net monthly income	−$ 3,714	−$20,964
September income	$90,000	
Expenses	54,488	
Net monthly income	$35,512	$14,548

The calculations are then transferred to the budget form (Fig. 4.9). Parentheses are used on the budget form to indicate negative numbers.

All categories for each of the 12 months must be completed in order to arrive at estimated yearly totals.

Most managers prepare their budgets in December or January for the next school year. Those that are less fortunate do them earlier and those lucky few get to guess closer to the start of their fiscal year. A more accurate budget is possible when it is prepared nearer to the start of the fiscal year.

		JULY	AUGUST	SEPTEMBER	OCTOBER
SUPPLIES & MATERIALS	Est				
	Actual				
To Date	Est				
	Actual				
REPAIR & MAINTENANCE	Est				
	Actual				
To Date	Est				
	Actual				
TOTAL MONTHLY EXPENSE	Est	17250	24714	54488	56304
	Actual				
To Date	Est	17250	41964	96452	152756
	Actual				
NET MONTHLY INCOME	Est	(17250)	(3714)	35572	36696
	Actual				
YEAR TO DATE	Est	(17250)	(20964)	14548	51244
	Actual				

MSU is an Affirmative Action/Equal Opportunity Institution

FIG. 4.9. Lower portion of budget form containing estimated net monthly income figures.

SU Department of Residence Halls
TIMATED AND ACTUAL
VENUES AND EXPENSES UNDERWOOD HALL Cafeteria ☒ Snackshop ☐ School Year 1986-1987

MONTH →		JULY	AUGUST	SEPTEMBER	OCTOBER	(ETC)	(ETC)	TOTALS
INCOME	Est	0	21000	90000	93000			
	Actual	50						
To Date	Est	0	21000	111000	204000			
	Actual	50						
PERSONAL SERVICES	Est	13800	14003	18870	17499			
	Actual	13700						
To Date	Est	13800	27803	46673	66172			
	Actual	13700						
FRINGE BENEFITS	Est.	3450	3157	3218	3325			
	Acual	3425						
To Date	Est	3450	6601	9819	13144			
	Actual	3425						
FOOD SUPPLIES	Est	0	7560	32400	33480			
	Actual	0						
To Date	Est	0	7560	39960	73440			
	Actual	0						
TOTAL MONTHLY EXPENSE	Est	17250	24714	54488	56304			
	Actual	17125						
To Date	Est	17250	41964	96452	152756			
	Actual	17125						
NET MONTHLY INCOME	Est	(17250)	(3714)	35572	36696			
	Actual	(17075)						
YEAR TO DATE	Est	(17250)	(20964)	14548	51244			
	Actual	(17075)						

MSU is an Affirmative Action/Equal Opportunity Institution

FIG. 4.10. Portions of budget form including July actual figures.

Actual Income and Expenses

The next step in our sample budget is to record actual income and expenses. This will give us a chance to see how accurate the estimates were.

Sometime in the middle to the end of August we will receive July's financial report from the accounting office. It may look like this.

Income:		$50
Expenses:		
Personal services	$13,700	
Fringe benefits	3,425	
Food supplies	0	
Etc.		
Total expenses		$17,125
Net income		−$17,075

When we record the July actual income and expenses on the budget sheet it resembles Fig. 4.10.

Due to the $50 income, the payroll savings of $100 in labor and $25 in fringe benefits, Underwood Cafeteria has $175 more than budgeted.

MSU Department of Residence Halls
ESTIMATED AND ACTUAL
REVENUES AND EXPENSES   UNDERWOOD HALL   Cafeteria ☒
                                                   Snackshop ☐   School Year 1986-1987

MONTH →		JULY	AUGUST	SEPTEMBER	OCTOBER	(ETC)	(ETC)	TOTALS
INCOME	Est	0	21000	90000	93000			
	Actual	50	22000					
To Date	Est	0	21000	111000	204000			
	Actual	50	22050					
PERSONAL SERVICES	Est	13800	14003	18870	17499			
	Actual	13700	14200					
To Date	Est	13800	27803	46673	66172			
	Actual	13700	27900					
FRINGE BENEFITS	Est.	3450	3457	3218	3325			
	Actual	3425	3120					
To Date	Est	3450	6601	9819	13144			
	Actual	3425	6545					
FOOD SUPPLIES	Est	0	7560	32400	33480			
	Actual	0	8000					
To Date	Est	0	7560	39960	73440			
	Actual	0	8000					
TOTAL MONTHLY EXPENSE	Est	17250	24214	54488	56304			
	Actual	17125	25320					
To Date	Est	17250	41464	76452	152756			
	Actual	17125	42445					
NET MONTHLY INCOME	Est	(17250)	(3714)	35572	36696			
	Actual	(17075)	(3320)					
YEAR TO DATE	Est	(17250)	(20464)	14578	51244			
	Actual	(17075)	(20375)					

MSU is an Affirmative Action/Equal Opportunity Institution

FIG. 4.11.   Portions of budget form including July and August actual figures.

FIG. 4.12. Portions of budget form including October actual figures.

Just before Labor Day the following August report arrives.

Income:		$22,000
Expenses:		
Personal services	$14,200	
Fringe benefits	3,120	
Food supplies	8,000	
Etc.		
Total expenses		$25,320
Net income		−$ 3,320

The budget sheet, Fig. 4.11, shows the actual figures for July and August. The budget, estimated last year is compared to actual income and expenses through October in Fig. 4.12. This is the information necessary for adjusting the budget so that it will balance at the end of the year. Now it is time for a review.

PERIODIC BUDGET REVIEW

A budget should not be etched in stone, rather it should be updated periodically in order to meet the needs of the organization. If income is running ahead of what was budgeted, there should be flexibility to increase some expenses. On the other hand, if the dish machine breaks down and has to be replaced, some other expense has to be cut or income has to be increased.

Ideally a review of the budget should take place monthly. The following questions should be considered. (1) Are income expectations being reached? (2) Are expenses, in total and by categories, similar to what was projected? If there are problems in either area what actions should be taken?

A major review and a revised budget should be made at the end of the first and second quarter, if the school is on a quarter system or in November and February for those schools on the semester system. If the budget is as projected the manager can sit back and smile. However, most of the time this will not be the case. There are too many variables, some controllable, some not, which affect the budget.

Some expenses are so small that they are almost not worth considering. Going back to the telephone example, the base rate was between $80 and $86 per month for a total budget of $1,238. By eliminating half of the telephones in the operation we could save $500. When compared to a total budget of a million dollars, this would be insignificant. The $500 would equal a 40% savings in the telephone bill, but would save only 0.05% of the total expenses. This does not mean that a review should not be made of the telephone system and cuts made where possible, rather it means a lot of time should not be spent on the minor categories.

There may be some categories that you have absolutely no control over such as fringe benefits, wage rates and administrative overhead. These will depend on the policies of the administration.

The cost of food and labor are the two categories over which the manager will have the most control. In both there are two functions to perform: (1) precosting food, the menu and labor; and after the fact (2) obtaining actual food and labor cost reports. The concept of precosting will be addressed first.

PRECOSTING

There are a number of computer programs available for precosting food and labor. These programs do more than just calculate the costs: they extend recipes, place orders with suppliers, print worksheets for cooks and much more. Since most foodservice operators spend a lot of time doing calculations, these programs are extremely valuable to them.

Precosting without a Computer

To understand what these programs can do for the supervisor, let us follow the steps that would have to be completed in order to use the precosting concept without computers.

The first step in precosting the food is to determine how many portions of each menu item are going to be served. This must be done on a daily basis. For example a menu has three entrees—beef stew, fried chicken and shrimp salad. Records show that when this combination is offered, students historically have taken them in these proportions: beef stew, 40%; fried chicken, 50%; shrimp salad, 10%.

In multiplying these percentages by our anticipated meal count of 450, the following serving projections were made: beef stew, 180; fried chicken, 225; shrimp salad, 45.

These figures are used to determine the amount of ingredients that need to be ordered. The amount of each ingredient needed to prepare each entree is listed for 100, 200 and 300 servings in the recipe file. The supervisor can multiply the 100-serving recipe by 1.8 or multiply the 200 recipe by 0.90 to obtain the quantity needed for 180 persons.

The amount of each ingredient is totaled, inventory of the storeroom is taken and those ingredients not on hand are ordered. The procedure can be summarized as follows:

1. Calculate how many orders are going to be needed.
2. From recipes, calculate raw ingredient needs.
3. Take inventory of what is on hand.
4. Subtract ingredient needs from inventory.
5. Place orders for items not on hand.
6. Print recipes for the cooks to use.

You would probably do this as a classroom project in a quiet corner of the library or in a locked room so there are no interruptions. However, in a real foodservice operation, this isolation is unrealistic. There are many ways to be sidetracked—the dish machine is overflowing—Peter does not show up—the cooks are falling behind in their work—people are interrupting constantly with questions. Some problems can be solved at the desk, but many require that the supervisor leave the office. Consequently, unless the manager is very organized, costly mistakes in calculations can be made. Halfway through the calculation of the beef stew recipe for 200 figured at 90% (to get 180 orders) the supervisor is interrupted. Returning to the office the person may be ordering not at 90%, but forget and calculate ingredients for the full 200 servings. That means foods will be purchased that are not necessary.

On the other hand if the other mistake is made and orders are calculated at 90% of 100 servings, the cooks will be upset as there will not be enough ingredients.

At other times whole menu items may be overlooked, or they may be repeated and the supervisor will order twice as much as needed. Orders will be late, not legible, short, and on and on.

Computer Precosting

The modern solution to this problem is the use of a computer. A precosting-ordering system is a time saver and can eliminate many mistakes. Recipes are entered into the computer; in some cases there might be five or six recipes for similar menu items. For example, there could be a regular beef stew, Irish beef stew, Texan beef stew, hobo beef stew and (if there is such a thing) meatless beef stew. By numbering each, they become separate recipes on the file and can be calculated as individual entrees.

With this new type of ordering system the supervisor enters into the computer the information for next Tuesday. Recipe no. B-150 is planned for 40% of the dinner guests (180 servings), and nos. C-212 for 50% (225 servings) and S-33 for 10% (45 servings). The computer prints the recipes with the correct amounts of each ingredient that are necessary for the servings required. The calculations are perfect; nothing is missed nor calculated twice. Recipes for all three items are printed, giving the correct quantities for the cooks to prepare.

The order forms are printed, listing each ingredient item and the quantities needed. The supervisor, taking inventory of the storage area to determine needs, has a check list. If interruptions occur it is a simple matter to continue without losing track.

Recipes are printed with the same format each time, and the cooks do not have to do any calculations. They will not have to read recipes handwritten by two or three different supervisors or typed by a clerk who has possibly made a mistake.

The speed and accuracy of the computer allows more time for supervisors to do what their title implies—to supervise.

Precosting a Menu by Computer

With the recipes on the computer it is easy to calculate portion costs. For example, Table 4.2 lists six beef stew recipes, four with different ingredients, and two with different portion sizes. A 6-oz portion is served in residence halls.

TABLE 4.2.   Beef Stew Recipes

Recipe #	Name	Portion size (oz)	Cost/ portion ($)
B-150	Beef stew, regular	6	0.60
B-152	Beef stew, regular	8	0.80
B-155	Beef stew, hobo	6	0.57
B-160	Beef stew, Irish	6	0.61
B-162	Beef stew, Irish	8	0.81
B-165	Beef stew, Texan	6	0.64

TABLE 4.3. Precosting Tuesday Dinner

Entree	Recipe (no.)	Cost/ portion ($)	Count (no.)	Total cost ($)
Beef stew	B-150	0.60	180	108
Fried chicken	C-212	0.52	225	117
Shrimp salad bowl	S-33	0.61	45	27
			450	252

Average cost per person $0.561

The catering service uses a 6-oz portion for luncheons and an 8-oz portion for evening banquets.

Precosting next Tuesday night's dinner is easy. The computer can be updated on the costs of ingredients on a frequent basis. This in turn calculates portion costs. Of the 450 students eating, 40% or 180 are expected to eat beef stew. Therefore, if recipe no. B-150 is scheduled, the simple calculation is 180 × $0.60 = $108. The precost of that entree is $108. The precost total of the three entrees planned for Tuesday night is given in Table 4.3. An average cost per person has been calculated as $0.561.

Precosting can be calculated on as many items of the menu as desired. The items most important for cost control are (1) entrees, (2) desserts, (3) salads, (4) soups, and (5) vegetables.

Other items, such as crackers, condiments and cereals, add to the cost of the operation, but generally are not the financial backbreakers.

The computer can be programmed to revise portion costs every week, every other week or once per month. Revisions should be scheduled as frequently as ingredient costs change. For example, in recipe no. B-150, regular beef stew, at $0.60 for a 6-oz serving, if stew meat goes up $0.16 per pound and the recipe contains one-third beef, the new portion cost will change from $0.60 to $0.62 as follows:

1. 6-oz serving contains 2 oz beef;
2. $0.16 increase per pound is a $0.01 per oz increase;
3. 2 oz ($\frac{1}{3}$ × 6 oz) in this serving is a $0.02 increase;
4. the old cost of the 6-oz portion was $0.60; the increase of $0.02 gives us a new portion cost of $0.62.

Refer again to the precosting of the 180 servings. The old cost was $108. The new cost is $0.62 × 180 = $111.60, an increase of $3.60 or 3.33% for that entree next Tuesday.

Computer printouts of portion costs can be obtained in four basic formats: (1) numerical order of the recipe, (2) alphabetical listing by category, (3) decreasing price by category, and (4) increasing price by category. Examples of these formats are given in Table 4.4.

Earlier in this chapter a budget was established that set the food cost equal to 36% of the expected income. If the students pay a set price for room and board, it is easy to estimate the per meal income. The next step is to establish a menu that will cost a certain percentage of that income, in this case 36%. If $2.35 is charged for lunch, the estimated food cost is $0.36 \times \$2.35 = \$0.85$.

Enter into the computer the number of people expected to choose each menu item and the program will compute the average cost for each day's lunch. Our example shows that the lunch costs vary from $0.83 to $0.89 with an average cost of $0.86. This is $0.01 more than the $0.85 budgeted earlier.

Lunch costs	
Monday	$0.88
Tuesday	.83
Wednesday	.84
Thursday	.88
Friday	.84
Saturday	.86
Sunday	.89
Average	$0.86

It is not possible to meet the food cost goal every meal, every day. Probably the best that can be done is by the week. At the end of the school year the foodservice manager should have averaged $0.85 per day. Precosting gives the foodservice an idea of how it is going to do. The actual, after the fact, food and labor cost reports give the real figures. If the actual cost is running $0.87 per day then it is necessary to start selecting menu combinations that will precost from $0.81 to $0.83.

Precosting is used for two purposes: (1) to set up a menu within the budget, and (2) to allow the menu to be adjusted intelligently during the year so that food cost goals are attained.

In our example, lunch food cost is budgeted at $0.85 per day and the precosted menu is calculated at $0.86 for next Tuesday. It is easy to review the menu and substitute a less costly, yet comparable item. Suppose by looking over the historical information, the manager finds that half the students are projected to take chicken noodle soup. Data in Table 4.4 indicates that recipe no. 114 is $0.02 cheaper than recipe no. 115. By substituting recipe no. 114 for recipe no. 115, the savings of $0.02 for each serving will allow us to meet our budget of $0.85.

Precosting Labor

There is not much difference between precosting food and precosting labor. Actually it is easier to precost labor because the hourly rates remain constant whereas food costs fluctuate weekly.

TABLE 4.4. Formats for Recipe Portion Costs

1. Numerically by recipe number—soups

Recipe Number	Name	Cost per portion ($)
109	Cream of broccoli soup	0.06
110	Cream of vegetable soup	0.13
112	Peanut butter soup	0.10
114	Chicken noodle soup, canned	0.05
115	Chicken noodle soup	0.07
130	Vegetable soup, canned	0.06

2. Alphabetically by category—sandwiches

Recipe Number	Name	Cost per portion ($)
224	Cheeseburger on bun	0.32
210	Club sandwich	0.41
250	Fried clams on bun	0.51
235	Meat balls on bun	0.40
209	Spartan club sandwich	0.36
245	Tuna bagel	0.31

3. Decreasing price by category—sandwiches

Recipe Number	Name	Cost per portion ($)
250	Fried clams on bun	0.51
210	Club sandwich	0.41
235	Meat balls on bun	0.40
209	Spartan club sandwich	0.36
224	Cheeseburger on bun	0.32
245	Tuna bagel	0.31

4. Increasing prices by category—soups

Recipe Number	Name	Cost per portion ($)
114	Chicken noodle soup, canned	0.05
109	Cream of broccoli soup	0.06
130	Vegetable soup, canned	0.06
115	Chicken noodle soup	0.07
112	Peanut butter soup	0.10
110	Cream of vegetable soup	0.13

TABLE 4.5. Labor Budget Form

	Hours		Dollars	
Labor category	Regulars	Students	Regulars	Students
Supervising				
Baking				
Cooking				
Salads				
Desserts				
Storeroom				
Dish room				
Serving				
Bussing–Dining room				
Ticket checking				
Custodial				
Clerical				

A labor budget should be established based on the previous year's figures. The budget should include both hour and dollar amounts because it is difficult to compare dollars from one year to the next with employees receiving wage and merit increases. A better basis of comparison is possible when the number of hours is used.

Computers help keep categories separate and calculate a variety of totals for both hour and dollar amounts. Labor categories are listed in Table 4.5.

The first step in calculating labor costs is to determine the number of regular employees hours needed in each category. Add to that the number of hours for part-time student employees.

Daily payroll is calculated by multiplying the wage rate of each employee or group of employees by the hours scheduled. Each day should be calculated individually, then totaled for the week's labor budget.

After precosting labor hours and dollars it is fairly easy for the manager to compare actual figures to the budget.

On a daily basis, keep an account of the hours; the dollars will take care of themselves. This is a little different than food cost. Food items have a very high degree of cost variance. Wages, except by classification (cooks vs. line servers vs. storeroom personnel, etc), will remain basically the same. As an example, the cost of a portion of beef stew in October might be very different in May. On the other hand, one hour's wages for a cook in October will probably be the same in May.

Track the number of hours spent in each labor category against what was budgeted. If the hours are in line the dollars spent will probably also be within budget.

ACCOUNTING REPORTS—ACTUAL AFTER THE FACT

Everything we have done so far has been "pre." A budget was established and the menus set up and precosted to meet the budget. Prior to ordering, the menu was again precosted (ingredient costs change each week) and now the meal is over. How did we do? Up until this point it was all guess work. Intelligent guess work, but still guess work.

Food Cost Reports

Most schools have a monthly accounting system with the financial statements reaching the operating units sometime between the twentieth and twenty-fifth of the following month.

Let us follow a typical school's accounting time table that is on the quarter system. School starts between the middle and the end of September. That means the foodservice manager receives the first financial report between the middle and the end of October. This 2-week report is not much help in reviewing the budget. The first 2 weeks are always a time of confusion and adjustment. There are a number of start-up costs; leftovers probably have not been used to their maximum; cooks are still trying to figure out what and when students are going to eat; students are tired of cooking for themselves over the summer and are eating more; plate waste is high; and on and on.

That means we have to wait until the October financial statement is published to get an idea of how we are doing. October is a good month, since there are four solid weeks of operation. The 1–2 weeks of getting organized are behind us, and there are no vacation periods or holidays to confuse the calculations. The only problem is that the report for October will not be ready until the middle of November or until as late as Thanksgiving week. By the time we can analyze the report, school has one week of classes and a week of finals left in fall term. The figures are great for historical records but practically useless from an operation standpoint. The fall term is over, and for schools on a quarter system that marks the end of one-third of the year.

One point a lot of new supervisors overlook is if an operation is halfway through a term or a year and, as an example, if the budget is running $10,000 over, it is necessary to cut spending by twice that amount ($20,000) for the last half of the period in order to attain a balanced budget. The sooner the problem is discovered, the easier it is to correct.

As an example, food cost is budgeted at $90,000 for the 9-month school year. At the end of 3 months actual costs are $40,000 as shown in the accompanying tabulation.

	Budget	Actual
First quarter	$30,000	$40,000
Second quarter	30,000	
Third quarter	30,000	
	$90,000	

The immediate reaction by a novice supervisor is to try and trim $10,000 from the current spending rate for the remainder of the year. This supervisor suggests cutting back $5,000 during each quarter to get on the right track. This will not work, because at the $40,000 pace if $5,000 is cut the actual cost will be $111,000 and not the original budgeted cost of $90,000.

Revised Budget 1	
First quarter (actual)	$40,000
Second quarter	35,000
Third quarter	35,000
	$110,000

To hit our budget the $5,000 has come off the original $30,000 estimate.

Revised Budget 2	
First quarter (actual)	$40,000
Second quarter	25,000
Third quarter	25,000
	$90,000

Timely Food Cost Reports

In order to get information when you need it, it might be necessary to set up a separate report outside of the college or university central financial accounting network. This can be accomplished either by having a separate computer or having the accounting office prepare an unofficial food cost report.

In a timely report the cost and quantity of some food items might be taken from the delivery tickets and not from the suppliers' invoices. Freight charges might be added later; pricing errors corrected when accounting verifies them. A big problem could be that the school's monthly statement may not take into account inventory that is in the foodservice storerooms and coolers. These are just some of the reasons why the food cost report and the official report might differ.

Financial Statements

Three monetary figures are needed to get started on an accurate food cost report: (1) beginning inventory, (2) purchases and (3) ending inventory.

By feeding this information into a computer, along with the number of meals served for breakfast, lunch and dinner food cost report can be prepared. Such a report should arrive fast enough to allow time for adjusting operations. An income and expense report that arrives within 7 to 10 days gives the operator enough time to adjust. The report should contain at least a weekly plus a to-date statement. Some schools use a to-date statement starting with the fiscal year. If the fiscal year starts 1-2 months before the beginning of fall term, a school may want to run a summer report and then start a school year report with the first week of school, allowing units to be compared on an even basis. Most schools only operate their halls periodically in the summer. Also some units spend a lot more labor on major repairs than do others. If the summers are included in the to-date section, it is a memory game in January and February. Who was open? Who had a large conference? Who had a lot of major work done?

The foodservice managers of the closed or open units may try to use that as an excuse for a high labor cost, high food cost, high laundry cost, etc. By eliminating the summer operations from the to-date report and starting everyone the first week of fall term, all foodservices are on an even-comparison basis.

A school should have the computer programmed to supply each manager with a very detailed report on his/her own operations as well as highlights of similar units on campus. The central administration should get a report of prime costs on all units. Prime costs are usually divided into four categories: (1) food, (2) labor, (3) supplies and (4) others (everything else). For example, each week the administration and the three unit managers may receive a comparison report that contains weekly and year-to-date figures (Table 4.6).

The report sent to each operating unit can be as simple or as detailed as the manager requests. Items have to be precoded and the more categories there are, the more coding is necessary. Also, the larger the number of categories, the greater the possibility that items will be put into the wrong group.

When the number of categories increases, so does the decision making. Does frozen liver go into the meat or frozen category? Are canned carrots in the staples or produce category? The key to categories is making sure all units are the same.

Six basic food categories recommended for a food cost report are (1) bakery,

TABLE 4.6.   Prime Cost Summary Week 27th and Year to Date

	Unit A		Unit B		Unit C		Average	
	Week	YTD	Week	YTD	Week	YTD	Week	YTD
Food	36.25	36.01	35.95	36.41	37.24	36.89	36.48	36.10
Labor	34.25	33.64	32.89	33.21	33.02	33.04	33.39	33.30
Supplies	3.95	4.02	8.64	4.08	2.75	4.11	5.11	4.07
Other	25.55	26.33	22.52	26.30	26.99	26.96	25.02	26.53
Total	100%	100%	100%	100%	100%	100%	100%	100%

(2) dairy, (3) frozen, (4) meat, (5) produce, and (6) staples. Some of these could be subdivided, but too many would be time consuming and serve no useful purpose.

In establishing categories think along these lines—"I have a food cost–labor cost of X% to meet. How many categories do I need to watch and control in order to meet that figure?"

FINAL REPORTS

If the record keeping has been adequate, the preparation of a final report will be easy. The final report could be a completed budget form for the entire year including the actual and estimated figures for all income and expense categories. The year-to-date figures will show whether or not the budget was met.

REFERENCES

AXLER, B. H. 1979. Foodservice: A Managerial Approach. NIFI, Chicago, IL.

BIRCHFIELD, J. Foodservice Operations Manual. CBI Publishing Co., Boston, MA.

BROWN, D. R. The Restaurant Managers Handbook. Atlantic Publishing Co., Silver Springs, FL.

CLOYD, F. 1972. Guide to foodservice management. Institutions Volume Feeding Magazine. Des Plaines, IL.

KAHRL, W. L. 1977. Advanced Modern Food and Beverage Service. Prentice–Hall, Englewood Cliffs, NJ.

KING, C. A. 1980. Professional Dining Room Management. Hayden Book Co., Saddle Brook, NJ.

NRA. 1982. How to Prepare a Restaurant Operations Manual. National Restaurant Association, Chicago, IL.

TOLVE, A. P. 1984. Standardizing Foodservice for Quality and Efficiency. AVI Publishing Co., Westport, CT.

5 Food Conservation

The amount of food wasted by people living in the United States is horrendous. There is food waste in this country at every step in the food chain: growing, storing, transporting, processing, selling, preparing, consuming and disposing of leftovers.

In many parts of the world there is no such thing as a garbage disposal because there is no garbage. Our society condones and, in many instances, encourages the wasting of food. We eat more than our daily requirements. If the food has an off flavor, or too much seasoning, or we just do not like the taste, it is discarded. Leftovers are often thrown out. If an apple or peach has a bad spot, the total fruit is discarded. If there is a little food left at the end of the meal, it is disposed of because it will not feed the whole family.

Students under an all-you-can-eat board plan have the attitude that "I have paid for the food and I can do what I want with it." The attitude prevails that food is a right and "what I do with my share is my business, not yours. I missed breakfast three times last week and the school owes me this food."

FOOD ECOLOGY PROGRAM

In the middle 1970s, Ted Smith, coordinator of foodservices at Michigan State University, jointly developed a food ecology program with Coca-Cola USA to make students aware of food waste and to combat rising campus food costs. The awareness campaign was developed with the help of Indiana University,

FIG. 5.1. Waste not award.

Yale University, the University of Illinois, Oklahoma State University, Oklahoma University, Ohio State University and Georgia Institute of Technology. Campaign materials included posters, table tents, contest suggestions and buttons. The messages were "Stop food waste—take only what you'll eat," "If you want less, tell me," "Butter is frequently wasted," "Milk is filling," and "Be a food ecologist."

In some schools, waste-not awards were handed to students in the dining rooms giving them a free 12-oz Coke when they became members of the clean plate club (Fig. 5.1). Other schools gave out lottery tickets to clean plate club members and had drawings once a week giving the winner a free pizza.

Food waste programs are similar to safety and sanitation programs in that they cannot just be run for a short period of time. Good results require that constant attention be given to the program. To make a food waste or ecology program totally effective, it is necessary to do a study before and after the program is run. By measuring the amount of wasted food prior to the program and again after the program is instituted, the success of the campaign can be determined. Schools across the country, depending on size, have realized savings of from $30,000 to $230,000 per year after running ecology campaigns.

AN INFORMAL PROGRAM

Run your own awareness or ecology program. Starting today, and ending 3 days from now, watch what your friends waste. What perfectly good food gets discarded? If you are living in a residence hall with an all-you-can-eat board plan, it will be a real eye opener.

Concentrate your observations on those foods that people already know the flavor of. Examples of foods with a known taste are bread, butter, margarine, yogurt, cottage cheese, crackers, canned fruits, carrot sticks, lettuce and beverages. (Also do not forget the ecology of the trees in our forests. Count the number of wasted napkins.)

One of the problems with doing a campaign on wasted food is the feeling by some disgruntled students that if the food were edible they would not waste so much. By concentrating on foods with a known taste such as those just listed, this comment is no longer valid. Unless there is a bad batch of yogurt or cottage cheese, every student should know the flavor of these foods, In a foodservice operation a more formal survey should be made.

FORMAL PROGRAMS

Have the dishroom workers save all the milk that is wasted during a given day. Empty all partially filled glasses into a bucket. Measure the amount of milk wasted for the entire day and put a money figure on the waste. Multiply that amount times the days in the week, the term or the school year. The larger the amount the bigger the impression on the students.

Five cents per day per student does not sound like much, but for a school of 2000 it would amount to $100 per day, $700 per week, $3200 per month and, depending on the number of school days, somewhere around $22,000 per year.

The study before the program should be conducted without the knowledge of the clientele. Gather the facts on several items, then start a campaign to make the students aware of the waste. Near the end of the campaign, repeat the study. Recalculate the costs to see what the savings are, and publish the results to the students. Thank them for their help in keeping costs down, and give them a banana split night, steak night or apple pie a la mode as a reward. In all probability the savings will pay for a number of treats.

Each cafeteria in a multi-unit operation will have different amounts of savings. How attractively the food is displayed, where it is in relation to other foods and how easy it is to obtain seconds or half portions will have an influence on waste.

If food is eye-appealing, the old adage "your eyes are bigger than your stomach" comes into play. At Michigan State University we studied two halls of a similar size, each with a different setup. One hall had desserts on the serving line and salads in the dining room, the other had the reverse. We experienced twice as much waste when the food was on the serving line. In most of our cafeterias desserts are not on the serving lines. They are available, but students must make an effort to get them and will not choose them on an impulse basis.

Impulse selection can cause waste. Students see an attractive dessert and take one, thinking they will want it by the end of the meal. After eating their salad, entree, vegetables and bread they no longer want the dessert. Some may pick at the dessert before discarding it. Others may eat all of the dessert but not really want it. The food wasted in the first dessert example is measurable, the amount in the second cannot be calculated.

A program for measuring plate waste can be as simple as collecting unused butter pats or crackers in the dish room or as complicated as a full-fledged weighing and measuring program.

Disseminating the results to the students can be as easy as displaying a pile of butter or crackers in the serving area with a sign reading "Based on yesterday's waste, this is how much will go down the garbage disposal this school year. Do not waste—it costs *you* money."

An example of a more elaborate program was one developed in 1977 by the Human Resources Institute for the Coca-Cola Company in affiliation with the Reading, Pennsylvania, branch of the American Association of University Women. Their program set out to determine plate waste by measuring: (1) the amount of plate waste per person served, and (2) the amount of waste as a percentage of total food served.

DAILY FOOD WASTE SURVEY

period   school   location

QUANTITY SERVED MENU ITEM	SERVING WEIGHT (OZ)	X	NO. OF SERVINGS	÷ 16 =	TOTAL WEIGHT (LB)
1					
2					
3					
4					
5					
6					
7					
8					
9					
10					
				TOTAL	A

TOTAL NUMBER OF PEOPLE	B

FIG. 5.2.   Daily food waste survey form in which serving portions are weighed.

DAILY FOOD WASTE SURVEY

date   meal   location

QUANTITY SERVED MENU ITEM (UNITS)	QUANTITY PREPARED (OZ)	—	QUANTITY UNSERVED (OZ)	÷ 16 =	TOTAL SERVED (LB)
1					
2					
3					
4					
5					
6					
7					
8					
9					
10					
			TOTAL	A.	

TOTAL NUMBER OF PEOPLE SERVED   B.

PLATE-WASTE MEASURED

CONTAINER DESCRIPTION		WEIGHT (LB) LESS CONT. WT	waste per person: (average)
WEIGHT	CONTENTS		$16C/B$ = _____ OZ
			percentage:
	TOTAL	C	C/A = _____ %

FOOD ITEMS MOST WASTED TODAY

COMMENTS:

SIGNED

FIG. 5.3.   Daily food waste survey form in which prepared food is weighed.

WEEKLY PLATE WASTE SUMMARY NO. _____

number of meals: _____   meals: _____   location: _____

DAILY TOTALS: MEAL NUMBER	TOTAL SERVED (LB)	PEOPLE SERVED	TOTAL PLATE WASTE	WASTE PER PERSON	WASTE % OF TOTAL
1					
2					
3					
4					
5					
6					
7					
8					
9					
10					
11					
12					
13					
14					
15					
16					
17					
18					
19					
20					
21					

TOTALS   A: _____   B: _____   C: _____

WEEKLY AVERAGE PER PER PERSON $16 \, C/B$ = _____ OZ

WEEKLY AVERAGE PER LB. FOOD SERVED C/A = _____ %

COMMENTS:

_____

SIGNED

FIG. 5.4.   Form for weekly summary of plate waste.

SEMIANNUAL FOOD WASTE SURVEY

| date | school | location |

WEEK (SPECIFY DATES)	NO. WEEKS	TOTAL SERVINGS	% WASTE PER PERSON
	1		
	2		
	3		
	4		
	5		
	6		
	7		
	8		
	9		
	10		
	11		
	12		
	13		
	14		
	15		
	16		
	17		
	18		
	19		
	20		
	21		
	22		
	23		
	24		
	25		
	26		

AVERAGE WASTE PER PERSON [   ] %

SIGNED _____

FIG. 5.5. Semiannual food waste form.

ANNUAL FOOD WASTE SURVEY
PROGRESS GRAPH-% WASTE PER PERSON

year   school   location

AVERAGE MONTHLY WASTE (%)	JAN	FEB	MAR	APR	MAY	JUN	JUL	AUG	SEP	OCT	NOV	DEC
50												
49												
48												
47												
46												
45												
44												
43												
42												
41												
40												
39												
38												
37												
36												
35												
34												
33												
32												
31												
30												
29												
28												
27												
26												
25												
24												
23												
22												
21												
20												
19												
18												
17												
16												
15												
14												
13												
12												
11												
10												
9												
8												
7												
6												
5												
4												
3												
2												
1												

FIG. 5.6. Annual food waste form.

The three figures needed to calculate the results are

1. Pounds of food served
2. Number of people served
3. Pounds of plate waste

The pounds of food served can be calculated in one of two ways: (1) by measuring the serving weight of the portion and multiplying this by the number of servings (Fig. 5.2), or (2) by weighing food prepared and subtracting the weight of food left over (Fig. 5.3). The number of people served is obtained from the line count. The method of calculating average waste per person and average percentage waste per person is indicated in the lower part of the plate waste form in Fig. 5.3.

Determining the pounds of plate waste is the hardest part of this program. The dish room crew must be well organized and do extra work. Buckets and bags of leftover food must be collected and weighed after each meal. Paper must be separated from garbage and if the meat has a bone, the bone removed before weighing. Some schools use a sampling technique. In lieu of measuring the waste on all trays, a 10 or 20% sampling is taken. So if the unit serves 600 students, a sample of 60 to 120 trays could be selected and the results extended for the full house count. Weekly, semiannual and annual food waste summaries are recorded on forms displayed in Figs. 5.4, 5.5 and 5.6, respectively.

WWOW Campaign

Miami University in Oxford, Ohio, developed a Waging War on Waste (WWOW) program in the mid 1970s.

The WWOW campaign was laid out step by step for all halls to follow:

Week beginning	WWOW activity
September 14	Initial waste measuring in the dining units. Specific schedule will be determined later.
September 26	Table tent: WWOW is coming (all freshman halls). Display September 27 and 28 (Fig. 5.7).
October 10	Table tent: Present results of measuring waste (all halls). Display October 12–14 (Fig. 5.8). WWOW buttons worn by all employees on serving line, at the check stands, and in the dining rooms, and managers (anyone around the students). WWOW napkins available at dinner, Wednesday, October 12.
October 17	WWOW poster displayed in all dining units for the week: "If you only want a small portion, ask for it." WWOW buttons worn by employees.
October 24	WWOW poster displayed in all dining units for the week: "Please take all you want . . . but eat what you take." WWOW buttons worn by employees.
October 31	WWOW poster displayed in all dining units for the week: "If you do not know what something is, ask for a sample." WWOW buttons worn by employees. WWOW napkins available at lunch, Wednesday, November 2.

WWOW Stands for WAGING WAR ON WASTE

Seven years ago the Department of Residence Halls initiated a WWOW Program. This program was started because many students and the Department of Residence Halls were concerned over the amount of food left on student trays. A plan was implemented to weigh and cost out food that was left on trays. A check on food waste in all dining halls was made during the lunch periods on September 12 through September 16 last year.

Total number of trays analyzed   975
Average weight of food waste per tray   3.35 oz
Average cost of food waste per tray $0.085

We will serve approximately 2,405,859 lunch and dinner meals this year. This costly waste at these meals could amount to $204,498 for the year! We will again analyze trays as they come in dishrooms.

Please save money and take only what you intend to eat; we will try to do our part through careful preparation and portion control.

Thank you!

FIG. 5.7.   Table tent for WWOW campaign.

November 7   Second waste measuring in the dining units. Specific schedule will be determined later.

November 28   Table tents: Results of second waste measuring (all halls). Display November 29–December 2. WWOW napkins available at dinner Thursday, December 1.

There is a cost to running a food waste campaign such as WWOW. Miami of Ohio, in addition to labor, had costs for special napkins, table tents and buttons. The amount of savings far outweighed the cost of the food waste program.

PROGRAM RESULTS

One school measured the liquid and solid waste in an 800-student residence hall. The results of the 7-day test are given in Table 5.1.

Table 5.2 shows the results of another study in which two halls, each housing 1100 students, had similar serving arrangements except that one (hall A) had desserts on the serving line and salads in the dining room, and the other (hall B) had the reverse. It can be seen that the most waste occurred when the food was on the serving line (i.e., more dessert was wasted in hall A and more salad wasted in hall B). This is a perfect example of the principle described earlier about having food accessible, but in such a position so as to avoid impulse choosing.

Congratulations!!!!!!
You're WWOW!!!

Yes, you're helping **W**in the **W**ar **O**n **W**aste!!! A second check of food waste left on trays was made in all dining halls in November. The *menus and number of trays analyzed were identical* to the first test in September. The second analysis shows a definite savings in food waste.

Comparison results

	September	November	Decrease
No. of trays analyzed	975	975	
Food waste per tray	3.35 oz	2.87 oz	14%
Cost of waste per tray	$.085	$.081	5%

Thank you for reducing food waste during the WWOW Campaign.

FIG. 5.8.A   WWOW results presented to students on this table tent (side 1).

The following chart shows facts concerning **Food Waste** on four self-service menu items common to each dining unit. We serve 2,405,859 lunches and dinners each year. At this rate of waste, the total waste and estimated dollar amount for the year is shown below.

November WWOW study	Milk	Other beverages	Salad bar	Cottage cheese
Average waste per tray	0.38 oz	0.617 oz	0.242 oz	0.091 oz
Total lb or 8-oz glasses	114,579	185,551	36,388	13,683
Total food cost waste	$10,999	$2,968	$12,226	$10,070

If we continue to achieve less food waste as reflected in the **WWOW Study** between September and November, a savings of 72,000 pounds of food would be realized. The savings will help contain room and board fees. *Please continue to be careful to not waste food.*

FIG. 5.8B.   WWOW results (side 2 of table tent).

TABLE 5.1. A 7-Day Plate Waste Study

Meal	Daily average	
	Solid (lb)	Liquid (gal)
Breakfast	8.00	4.75
Lunch	51.50	5.50
Dinner	75.75	6.00
Total	135.25	16.25

TABLE 5.2. A 5-Day Plate Waste Study

	Avg waste/ person/meal		Total liquid waste	
	Salads (oz)	Desserts (oz)	Breakfast juice (gal)	Milk and other bev. (gal)
Hall A	0.423	0.544	7.05	14.2
Hall B	0.788	0.389	8.30	17.4

TABLE 5.3. Oklahoma State Plate Waste Study

Resident hall	Food served[a] (lb)		Waste[a] (lb)		People served[a] (no.)		Plate waste[a] (%)		Avg waste/ person[a] (oz)	
A	933	955	192	151	1118	1143	20.5	15.8	2.75	2.11
B	699	662	135	87	755	771	19.3	13.1	2.86	1.81
C	1080	987	239	157	1025	991	22.1	15.9	3.68	2.53
D	407	373	91	58	426	424	22.4	15.6	3.42	2.19
E	652	587	109	92	654	609	16.7	15.7	2.66	2.42
F	1280	1150	254	210	1209	1187	19.8	18.3	3.36	2.83
G	308	218	46	31	279	224	14.9	14.2	2.64	2.21
Total	5359	4932	1066	786	5466	5349				
Average							19.9	16.0	3.12	2.43

[a]The first number in the column represents the data taken before the program began. The second number represents the results 7 weeks after the program was initiated.

Oklahoma State University conducted a survey in its seven residence halls on October 19, before a food ecology program was instituted and again on December 7, after the program had been in progress for 7 weeks. In every case (Table 5.3) there was less waste after the program had been instituted. The largest amount of waste was 22.4% in hall D before the program, and hall B had the least amount of food wasted (13%) after the program. The average waste per person was 3.12 oz before the campaign began and 2.43 oz afterwards. There was 280 lb (1066−786) less waste per day after the program had been underway for 7 weeks. This represents about one ton of food each week.

DO YOU NEED A PROGRAM?

The foodservice manager must analyze why food is being wasted and try to reduce that waste as much as possible. Are servings too large? Is the food cold, overcooked, overspiced or dried out? Are students taking seconds to get part of the food for another item (e.g., removing a bacon slice garnish from three entrees in order to make one bacon, lettuce and tomato sandwich, then discarding the remainder of the three entrees)?

If all of these situations are corrected and waste is still too high, then a food conservation campaign is needed. Remember, it is not enough to start a program, it must be continued through the years.

REFERENCE

HELDMAN, D. R. 1979. Food losses and wastes in the domestic food chain of the United States. National Service Foundation Report. DAR 76-80693, National Technical Information Services, Springfield, VA.

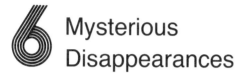 # Mysterious Disappearances

Unexplained loss of items or poor cost control can be lumped into one category and labeled mysterious disappearances. Although the stealing of food and other items is the most common cause of these disappearances, there are many others. Delivery and bookkeeping shortages, carelessness and accidents by employees resulting in lost or broken equipment and ruined food, improperly prepared food, poor portion control, poor inventory control and wasteful use of utilities, all can fall under the heading of mysterious disappearances.

THEFT

The most well-known mysterious disappearance, theft, is defined as the act of stealing. Many times the theft is direct, as when the employee takes food from the storeroom or freezer, or the student takes food or other items from the dining room. There are also hidden forms of theft. These include such things as employees calling in sick when they are not, having co-workers clock in for them or simply wasting time on the job.

Employee Theft

Employees have the best opportunity to steal. Most employees from the manager to the diswasher feel that they are underpaid. People can always find someone that has about the same job and makes more money. They might be able to find others that make less, but those are quickly forgotten and their minds focus on Don or Angie who has less responsibility and makes more money.

Student employees are convinced that they are overworked and underpaid. Tuition is too expensive, room and board is too costly and books are overpriced.

The employee thinks: "The company is underpaying me and they will not miss this pound of hot dogs, bottle of drain cleaner and package of paper clips. I need to mail this letter and need a stamp. The school will not miss one stamp."

Customer Theft

The hardest area to protect against stealing is the dining room. One of the students leaving the dining room takes a plate, glass, ash tray or some flatware. Maybe it is for a student room or next year's off-campus apartment. Whatever the reason the problem is the rationalization by the customers that they have been overcharged or cheated and the school owes them something. It could be that a student missed a number of meals or the food was cold last week and "I couldn't eat it." Therefore it is all right to take these items.

It is interesting that sometimes they cannot forget that they stole the items. Periodically, schools will receive a box of flatware or dishes from an ex-student with a note—usually anonymous—saying something like "I am sorry that I took this from the school. It has been bothering me for a couple of years. Enclosed is some stainless that belongs to Underwood Residence Hall." Unfortunately, the number of returned items do not approach the quantity of those that mysteriously disappear.

Cafeterias that have a cash register at the end of the line do not present the same psychological problems with food being taken out of the dining room as those with an all-you-can-eat board plan. In a cash operation, if a customer puts an apple in a pocket or knapsack, there is no doubt by anyone that this is stealing.

The distinction is not quite so clear in the case of the all-you-can-eat board plan. Policies vary in what and how much food can be taken out of the dining room. Some schools allow ice cream cones, others cereal, crackers or maybe a piece of fruit. In others absolutely nothing can be taken out of the dining room. Whatever the plan, it is based on what the school is charging the students for board.

A hypothetical illustration would be a school with a policy in one hall stating that (1) Each student may take $5 worth of food from the dining room every day; (2) No food may be taken out of the dining room at any time. It is easy to see that the first policy would result in an extra cost of $5 per day or $35 per week per student.

In both cases, however, the foodservice manager has calculated cost averages, based on the policy and determined board rates from that cost. Taking food from the dining room leads to a higher cost and therefore a higher charge to the students the next year.

A difficult concept to get across to students is that just because a student missed a meal yesterday or did not eat very much for lunch today, does not mean the student can take extra food out of the dining room tonight or sneak a freeloader in for lunch on Saturday. A student might think, "I paid for 13 meals and I only eat 12 each week. Therefore, I have the right to bring my friend in for lunch."

Schools that offer meal plans calculate the meal rates on expected absenteeism. Records indicate that a certain percentage of the students are going to miss meals and this information is built into the pricing for the meal plan. If every student ate every meal that they were entitled to, board charges would have to increase.

Back-of-the-House Theft

Another form of food stealing is theft by employees, passers-by or purveyors from the kitchen or back dock.

It is important to remove items from the back dock into the storeroom as quickly as possible. More raw food is lost to theft here than any place in the building. Items unattended on the back dock can disappear in a number of ways:

1. People passing by can just lift it off the delivery skid and keep walking.
2. Employees going home can either hide it for later pickup or carry it to their cars right away.
3. Purveyors can put it back on their truck and either take it home or sell it at the next stop.

Storerooms should be located inside the cafeterias under observation from the supervisor's office. Once the food is under lock and key it becomes more difficult to steal. This eliminates the possibility of theft by passers-by and purveyors.

It is very obvious when nonemployees are in the storeroom area and having the storeroom under observation makes it more difficult for them to steal. At the same time it also becomes more difficult for employees to steal, and if they do, harder to take large quantities as was possible when items were left unattended on the back dock.

Do not tempt delivery people to steal. Cluttered back docks lend themselves to truck drivers unloading and, after the storeroom person counts the supplies and signs the delivery slip, putting some of the goods back on the truck. A cluttered back dock indicates that there is confusion in the organization and that missed items will be written off as mysterious disappearances.

Vendor Theft

A scheme practiced by some drivers is to load onto their trucks items left on the dock by previous purveyors. With this type of theft, it is more difficult to trace the shortage, as schools will contact the supplier whose items are missing. Once the driver leaves, there is no way to tie him or her to the disappearance of the goods.

Watch for this behavior in drivers, it may indicate dishonesty.

1. Drivers lingering or hanging around after the delivery.
2. Drivers trying to sell you *specials* off the truck. Most companies do not do this and the special has probably been stolen from one of the earlier stops.
3. Drivers frequently not having the complete order, but when questioned finding your goods *misplaced,* or having fallen off the skid onto the floor.
4. Drivers always showing up at the same time as other deliveries. During times of confusion it is easier to take something.
5. The super-helpful driver—one that will take the items right to the store- room or refrigerator *just to help you.*

Another form of vendor theft is that of being shorted on deliveries. The most obvious theft by vendors is quantity shortages. For example, the requisition and invoice show that three cases have been ordered. But, only two are received, no corrections are made, and the school pays for the three. In some instances these are honest mistakes by the purveyors, but sometimes they know exactly what they are doing.

For example, the school pays for an order that includes white meat tuna, U.S. Choice beef and Grade A (Fancy) catsup; but light meat tuna, U.S. Good beef and Grade C (Standard) catsup were delivered.

Being invoiced at a higher rate than quoted by the salesperson is another form of vendor theft. This could be a deliberate act on the part of the supplier or maybe just a clerical mistake.

In order to keep vendor theft at a minimum, the person in charge of receiving the merchandise must check the quantity and quality of all items against the invoice and quoted prices. Only with careful attention to detail will costly errors be prevented.

SECURITY

Large-scale thefts usually occur during off hours. It is very difficult for some- one to take five cases of anything while the business is in operation. But when there are no supervisors around and it is night, stealing becomes much easier.

The secret to security after hours is locks and keys. Deadbolt locks are more secure than the push-button ones. Garbage and trash areas should be located inside the building and locked so employees cannot stash merchandise in them during the daytime, returning at night to pick it up.

Periodically, say every year, the list of who has keys to what should be reviewed, and the question asked, "does the employee need those keys?". The goal is to reduce the temptation to steal and at the same time protect employees from falling under suspicion of theft. If Jack or Chris do not have a key to the freezer, they cannot be accused of using it to take 30 pounds of hamburger. Equally important is that if the employee does not have a key, they are not tempted to return at midnight to take the food.

When reviewing the list of who has keys, ask the question, "do they need them on a regular and continuing basis?" If it is the job of an employee to open or lock up only when the regular person is on vacation, it is probable that the relief person does not need a key 365 days a year. It is much wiser to give the relief person the keys only when the regular person is on vacation.

One area not generally considered in discussing keys and security is the theft by a member of an employee's family. Employees that use keys infrequently sometimes do not carry them, but leave them at home unsecured. It is easy for a family member to *borrow* the key for a day or two, and no one will even realize it is gone.

There are some organizations that require their employees to leave keys at work when they are on vacation. It is not a good idea for employees to take keys on vacation trips, or even to leave them in their homes.

Another good security practice is to have all employees leave by one exit. This provides the employer with a means to observe what is being taken from the building. When employees leave the building they should show any boxes or shopping bags to a supervisor for inspection. The hardest part of this policy is getting it started. The "don't you trust me?" feeling by employees may make it difficult—but not impossible.

TIME IS MONEY

Stealing money and merchandise is considered a major crime by our society. Yet day in and day out some employees steal time from their employers, thinking it is clever, not criminal. Theft of time for some reason, is not considered really stealing. The employee that arrives late has a friend punch in the time card and therefore gets paid for time not on the job. Another employee wastes extra time in the bathroom, locker room or on the back dock. Through the payroll system, these extra breaks of 15 or 20 minutes are a form of stealing money from the school.

Most employees would never open the school safe and steal $2 or $3. Yet many would not hesitate stealing one-half hour or 8 hours of company time by goofing off or calling in sick when they are not.

Our society is very intolerant of theft of goods, supplies or cash, yet it becomes an internal disciplinary matter when it comes to company time.

CARELESSNESS

Theft is an active cause of mysterious disappearances. There is another, passive cause—carelessness. Every area of foodservice management can be affected by carelessness. The more carelessness, the more cost to your organization.

Lost Flatware and Broken Dishes

Carelessness with flatware in the dishroom or by the students in the dining room can lead to mysterious disappearance of those items. The school using garbage disposals rather than garbage cans have less of a problem. A fork in a garbage disposal will make more noise than one being tossed into a garbage can.

Restaurant supply companies sell magnetic equipment for use in the garbage collecting area. After the dishes are scraped, the garbage moves down a conveyor belt to either a disposal or can. A magnet installed over the belt, or a magnetized belt, will collect the metal flatware and prevent it from being damaged in the disposal or being tossed out in the garbage can.

Each year a lot of dishes must be replaced because they have been chipped, cracked or broken. If a customer drops a tray in the serving area, they may only break a glass or a dinner plate. If someone drops something in the dishroom it will be a stack of plates, or a rack of glasses, or a tray of coffee cups. Everyone laughs at the person for being careless, but it is not funny, it is costly.

The dishroom, where most breakage occurs, is a long, fast moving, sloppy area. The noise, activity and fast pace cause people to be less careful. Here is the area for a training program to be instituted.

Sliding one stack of dishes into another causes more damage than is imagined by the dishroom crew. The edges of one stack hit the other just right to cause a severe blow. Because the dishes are of different thicknesses, the edges do not meet evenly and they hit with a glancing blow. Chips are not noticed at that time as they may not fall off but remain intact until a jarring occurs later.

Another problem is that of cracking. When dishes, bowls and cups are damaged it is usually when they are being stacked. Bowls are a problem when the foot or base of the top bowl does not meet the inside bottom of the bowl underneath. Bowls and cups usually rest in a manner that causes strain on the sides of the pieces under them. Stress fractures occur at the time the dishes are stacked (at either end of the dish machine) or when they are transported across a bumpy tiled floor.

Stress fractures or cracks do not show up for a week or so. The dark line that is eventually seen by the customer is the fracture, filled with dirt, the dirt making the fracture visible.

ACCIDENTS

Mysterious disappearances due to accidents are generally in two areas: lost time and lost products.

Lost time, in the case of an employee being off work for a day or a week, is easily calculated. It is more difficult to calculate the labor time lost when a baker has to clean up spills or remake a sheet cake because someone accidently turned the oven off or accidently put sugar in the salt bin.

Accidents can cause lost time, from as little as five minutes for a cut finger which requires a bandage, to many hours or even days because of a severe injury. Lost time due to injuries is not only costly to the organization, but is also difficult for all involved. Whenever there is an injury, not only is the injured worker affected, but so is the entire organization. Co-workers must either increase their work load to cover for the injured person, or a temporary replacement has to be hired and trained. In addition, time is lost due to the disruption in the routine of daily work and overtime may be required. Mysterious disappearances of labor dollars may be nothing in a cut or scratch, but could be monumental in a serious accident.

The damage to equipment and the waste of food or supplies because of accidents is never calculated as a separate expense category. When a stack of china is dropped in the dishroom or at the serving line the cost will not show up as a separate item on the monthly statement; nor will the cost of food that is accidently dropped on the floor or oversalted and quickly put down the garbage disposal. Carelessness and accidents are often the result of poor training.

POOR TRAINING

Much time is wasted when employees are not trained to do their jobs properly. There are optimum ways to perform most tasks. The assembly line method of making sandwiches, or a systematic arrangement of items in a storeroom so that they are easily found are two examples.

In addition to time, wasting of supplies can also result from the lack of proper training. Large quantities of liquid supplies can be wasted if the so-called glug system—the most widely used form of chemical measuring—is allowed to become a common practice among workers.

The glug system is so named from the sound that the solution makes when a quantity of it pours out of the bottle and is replaced by air. Some jobs in foodservice require measurements of solutions from a container with a small opening.

Another common practice is to assign a new employee to one that has been on the job for a while. The combination of the buddy training system and the glug method can be very dangerous. The old employee shows the new one the ropes and explains that 2 glugs in the mop bucket or sink are the correct measurements.

A day or two later the new employee, doing the job alone, decides that if 2 glugs will do the job properly, then 3 will do it better. Careful training and supervision in the proper techniques will help minimize waste in this area.

The use of automatic dispensers to replace the glug system will save money. Without close supervision the proper amount of solution is dispensed. Training of new employees is minimal and they are less likely to make mistakes in measuring.

Some mysterious disappearance of food may be the result of poor training or insufficient supervision. Careless preparation, such as over- or under-cooking, poor seasoning or incorrect serving temperatures, can result in lost money. Customers will not select poorly prepared items. At the end of the meal, because of its poor quality, the food will be discarded, not even used as a leftover.

Improper Food Handling

Poor handling of food can lead to mysterious disappearances. This can be a real cost problem during all stages of the operation, starting with the receiving procedures and ending with service to the customer.

The receiving clerk can mishandle the items in a number of ways. Improper stacking leads to crushing items such as bakery goods and glass jars. Milk, meat, fish, vegetables and frozen items left out of the refrigerator or freezer will spoil quickly. When frozen foods thaw and are refrozen, they lose their quality and may have to be discarded.

The supervisor must be on the outlook for improper handling of food. For example, a cook who throws out spoiled meat may be a friend of the receiving clerk who should have taken better care of it. The supervisor may never know that the hamburger went down the garbage disposal instead of into the chili.

Some managers do not like garbage disposals. They prefer garbage cans so they can keep an eye on what is being thrown away. A cook or storeroom person can hide mistakes by discarding them in a garbage disposal but it is harder to hide mistakes in a garbage can.

Improper preparation can result in waste because food that does not look good will not be taken by the customer. Sometimes the poorly prepared item may also be the least expensive.

As an example, suppose the dinner offering is two entree selections: roast beef and macaroni and cheese. Past records show that 75% of the students take roast beef and 25% choose macaroni and cheese. If the macaroni and cheese is burned and only 10% of the students select it, that means 90% take the roast beef. The mysterious disappearance is the increased cost of serving 15% more roast beef, which is the high cost item.

Proper training in portion control is extremely important in reducing waste. There are many reasons why the server does not serve the proper amount. He or she may be partial to a certain student and will put twice as much goulash, chili or lasagna on the plate. The student line server may want to impress a boy or girl friend and give a little larger portion.

Most schools have a policy where extra servings are allowed and there is no reason for the server to give a larger portion to the customer. When 5.5 oz is served instead of 4.5 oz, there is a 22% mysterious disappearance. In many cases the customer does not want or need the extra food. The customer may leave some of it on the place and it gets discarded as garbage. In other cases the students may eat all of the food even if they do not want it.

An untrained server may have a perception problem and not realize that the customer is getting more than just the entree being placed on the plate. It may look like a small serving but with the bread, salad, dessert and beverage, it is a complete meal. Their visibility is limited to the large dinner plate with only the entree and the vegetable.

The serving personnel have to be constantly aware that hot food should be hot and cold food should be cold. Nothing is worse than soup that is cold or a hot roast beef sandwich that tastes like it has been in the refrigerator for two hours. After one or two bites the student that is hungry will get something else and the soup and sandwich will mysteriously disappear down the disposal.

Overproduction

If more of an item is prepared than is needed, leftovers result, and leftovers are always a problem. The first problem is storage; they must be covered, labeled and cooled properly. Second, what can be done with them? Most leftovers are not as good when served the second time. All foodservice establishments from the fanciest country club to the least expensive cafeteria use leftovers. To prevent mysterious disappearances, schools must use leftovers, too. Training will help cooks use leftovers efficiently and with imagination. The easiest way of controlling the use of leftovers is through careful planning and estimating needs.

MISUSE OF UTILITIES AND EQUIPMENT

Misuse of equipment is commonly found in kitchens. A cook uses a sharp knife as a can opener, a meat cleaver as a hammer or a table knife as a screwdriver. Expensive cloth napkins are sometimes used as rags for cleaning up. These habits result in lost money for the operation.

The misuse of equipment that does not belong to the school may not be perceived as an added expense. But the use of the local dairy company's milk cases or the laundry company's hampers raises their costs which in turn are passed on to their customers in increased rates. It is estimated that the misuse of milk cases in the state of Michigan costs dairy plants over $3,000,000 per year (see Fig. 6.1).

Another problem is the whole area of saving energy. When most colleges and universities were being built, conservation of gas, water, electricity and heat were of little concern. Today, the mysterious disappearances of energy supplies and water can lead to some high costs. A supervisor should review, on a regular schedule, all operations involving these utilities. Chances are there will be some waste that can be eliminated in this area. The largest savings will take place the first 2 years. After that the cuts will probably be less, but there will still be cuts.

A few areas to question during the review include the following.

1. Dish machine usage—is it turned on at 6 A.M. and off at 7 P.M. running idle for long periods of time during the day? Why not rinse and stack the breakfast dishes and start the machine a half hour before lunch? Is the machine functioning properly? Is the cleaning solution too strong? Is the water temperature too high?

2. Pot washing—is the water left running?

3. Lighting—are the lights always turned on when the first person arrives in the morning and off when the last person leaves? (Lights may be needed during the winter or on dark, stormy days, but during sunny weather all or some of the dining room lights could be turned off.) Are there too many light fixtures. If so, remove some bulbs or use lower wattage bulbs.

4. Refrigerator and freezer usage—are refrigerator doors left open for extended periods of time? Are there curtains missing from the cooler doors? Are the gaskets on all refrigerator and freezer doors in poor condition?

5. Ovens, ranges and serving counters—are ovens turned on to preheat too early? Are ranges kept on when not in use? Are serving counters kept on all the time?

6. Ventilation—are people opening and closing windows and doors unnecessarily? Are exhaust fans running unneeded 24 hours a day?

Large savings in heating and ventilating can be realized with the use of automatic timers. A timer installed on the equipment can turn it off and then turn

YOU
MAY BE IN POSSESSION
OF STOLEN PROPERTY
AND COULD BE FINED AS MUCH AS $500.^{00}

MISSING MILK CASES = $3,000,000.^{00}

Dairies in Michigan lose $3,000,000.^{00}
each year on mis-use of milk cases

WHERE DO THEY GO?

Garages/Residence Halls/School class rooms/Homes

Each year more than one and a half
million cases are pilfered and never
returned to the manufacturing plants

WARNING!

In accordance with the provisions of Act No. 222 of Public Acts of 1913
as amended and added to by Act No. 361, Public Acts of 1927, and Acts
of 1935, it is a **violation** of this Act to destroy, secrete or withhold milk
cases. Any person, firm or corporation so offending is liable and is guilty of
a **misdemeanor** punishable by a **fine** of not less than $50 and not more than
$500, or **imprisonment** for not more than **90 days,** or both.

DAIRY MANUFACTURERS DO NOT WANT TO RESORT TO
PROSECUTION FOR ILLEGAL USE OF MILK CASES.

WE JUST WANT OUR MILK CASES RETURNED.

If you have milk cases in your possession,
RETURN THEM TO ANY RESIDENCE HALL CAFETERIA.

FIG. 6.1. Missing milk case warning.

it back on at the optimal time each day. This eliminates the problem of regular or substitute people who forget to turn equipment on or off.

A timer can be preset to turn the heat down a half hour before the last person is scheduled to leave, and to turn the heat on prior to the arrival of the first person in the morning. Now the only thing the supervisor has to remember is to adjust the timer to changing work conditions. For example, during Thanksgiving break, winter break and spring break the hours of ventilation need to be adjusted. The school year schedule requires a different timing schedule than the summer one. A 7-day timer can also be used to shut the system off on weekends.

These are some of the small, yet important, things the supervisor can observe and correct. More complicated things like insulation, mixture of incoming and returning air and obsolete equipment should also be considered but the engineering department should be involved in this area.

POOR INVENTORY

Poor inventory can lead to either too much or too little stock. Both result in poor cost control. Perishable goods that are overstocked will spoil or if the food is used, the results may not be satisfactory and the resulting product will not sell. The money used to overstock the storeroom could be used for other purposes.

Understock causes more of an operational problem than a financial one. Nothing is more frustrating for the cooks and supervisors than to discover at the last minute that they are out of items needed. A change in the menu might be necessary.

Instead of changing the menu the manager may send an employee to a retail store to buy the needed food. This is costly, since the retail price is usually higher than the wholesale price. In addition, wages are paid for the employee to go to the store. Time was spent looking for the item in the storeroom, phoning various stores to locate the item and finally going after it.

Another way of handling the shortage is to call local wholesalers and ask them to make special deliveries. This might work once or twice, but not on a continuing basis. Pretty soon the manager will not be able to find any supplier to service the account.

In any foodservice operation there will be shortages from time to time. If it is a common occurrence then a review of the situation is in order. Good inventory procedures will keep the cost of the foodservice operations down.

SUMMARY

The problem with calculating mysterious disappearance costs is that they are hidden in the profit and loss statement. Each category of the financial report reflects mysterious disappearance costs in its total. The sharp manager watches for stolen, lost or wasted energy, food, labor and supplies and keeps mysterious disappearance costs to a minimum.

REFERENCES

AXLER, B. H. 1974. Security for Hotels, Motels, and Restaurants. ITT Educational Publishing, Indianapolis, IN/New York, NY.

CAS–OSHA. 1977. Kitchen Safety. Cal-OSHA. Dept. of Industrial Relations, 525 Golden Gate Avenue, San Francisco, CA.

CURTIS, B. 1975. Food Service Security: Internal Control. Lebhar-Friedman Books, New York, NY.

LENINGER, S. 1975. Internal Theft: Investigation and Control. Security World Publishing Co., Inc., Los Angeles, CA.

NSC. 1967. Hand Knives (bulletin). National Safety Council, 425 North Michigan Avenue, Chicago, IL.

UNKLESBAY, N., UNKLESBAY, K. 1982. Energy Management in Foodservice. AVI Publishing Co., Westport, CT.

7 Sanitation and Food Handling Techniques

From a pass/fail standpoint of any college or university foodservice, sanitation is the most important part of any day. Failing in sanitation can be devastating to the school and to the management staff.

Cleanliness and sanitation in a foodservice establishment are important both for appearance and for the prevention of food poisoning. A distinction should be made between the two terms: clean refers to the absence of dirt and debris, whereas sanitary refers to the absence of harmful organisms. A food preparation surface may look clean but be swarming with bacteria. It is clear to everyone when something is clean, but it is much harder to determine when something is sanitary. An example of this is a cutting board that is used to cut poultry and then, after being wiped clean, is used to cut vegetables for a salad. The bacteria from the poultry is left on the cutting board and because the board was not sanitized, the bacteria are transferred to the salad where they may multiply and lead to food poisoning.

CLEANLINESS

The first step in keeping high sanitation standards is being sure the entire foodservice operation is clean. Because dirt and litter carry microorganisms, a dirty kitchen will probably lead to sanitation problems.

The importance that public health people place on cleanliness in foodservice

DEPARTMENT OF HEALTH, EDUCATION AND WELFARE
PUBLIC HEALTH SERVICE · FOOD AND DRUG ADMINISTRATION

FOOD SERVICE ESTABLISHMENT INSPECTION REPORT

Based on an inspection this day, the items circled below identify the violation in operations or Facilities which must be corrected by the next routine inspection or such shorter period of time as may be specified in writing by the regulatory authority. Failure to comply with any time limits for corrections specified in this notice may result in cessation of your Food Service operations

OWNER NAME

ESTABLISHMENT NAME

ADDRESS

ZIP CODE

ESTABLISHMENT I.D.				CENSUS TRACT	SANIT CODE	DATE			INSPECT TIME (Min.)	PURPOSE		29
COUNTY	DISTRICT	TYPE	EST. NO.			YR.	MO.	DAY				
1 2 3	4 5 6	7 8 9	10 11 12	13 14	15 16	17 18	19 20 21	22 23 24	25 26 27 28	Regular 1	Complaint 3	

Follow-up 2   Investigation 4
Other 5

ITEM	WT	COL	ITEM	WT	COL	ITEM	WT	COL
FOOD			18 PRE-FLUSHED, SCRAPED, SOAKED	1	47	**GARBAGE AND REFUSE DISPOSAL**		
*01 SOURCE, SOUND CONDITION, NO SPOILAGE	5	30	19 WASH, RINSE WATER CLEAN, PROPER TEMPERATURE	2	48	33 CONTAINERS OR RECEPTACLES, COVERED, ADEQUATE NUMBER, INSECT/RODENT PROOF, FREQUENCY, CLEAN	2	62
02 ORIGINAL CONTAINER, PROPERLY LABELED	1	31	*20 SANITIZATION RINSE CLEAN, TEMPERATURE, CONCENTRATION, EXPOSURE TIME, EQUIPMENT, UTENSILS SANITIZED	4	49	34 OUTSIDE STORAGE AREA ENCLOSURES PROPERLY CONSTRUCTED, CLEAN CONTROLLED INCINERATION	1	63
FOOD PROTECTION			21 WIPING CLOTHS CLEAN, STORED, RESTRICTED	1	50	**INSECT, RODENT, ANIMAL CONTROL**		
*03 POTENTIALLY HAZARDOUS FOOD MEETS TEMPERATURE REQUIREMENTS DURING STORAGE, PREPARATION, DISPLAY, SERVICE, TRANSPORTATION	5	32	22 FOOD CONTACT SURFACES OF EQUIPMENT AND UTENSILS CLEAN, FREE OF ABRASIVES, DETERGENTS	2	51	*35 PRESENCE OF INSECT/RODENTS - OUTER OPENINGS PROTECTED, NO BIRDS, TURTLES, OTHER ANIMALS	4	64
*04 FACILITIES TO MAINTAIN PRODUCT TEMPERATURE	4	33	23 NON-FOOD CONTACT SURFACES OF EQUIPMENT AND UTENSILS CLEAN	1	52	**FLOORS, WALLS AND CEILINGS**		
05 THERMOMETERS PROVIDED AND CONSPICUOUS	1	34	24 STORAGE, HANDLING OF CLEAN EQUIPMENT/UTENSILS	1	53	36 FLOORS CONSTRUCTED, DRAINED, CLEAN GOOD REPAIR, COVERING INSTALLATION DUSTLESS CLEANING METHODS	1	65
06 POTENTIALLY HAZARDOUS FOOD PROPERLY THAWED	2	35	25 SINGLE-SERVICE ARTICLES STORAGE, DISPENSING, USED	1	54	37 WALLS, CEILING, ATTACHED EQUIPMENT CONSTRUCTED, GOOD REPAIR, CLEAN SURFACES, DUSTLESS CLEANING METHODS	1	66
*07 UNWRAPPED AND POTENTIALLY HAZARDOUS FOOD NOT RE-SERVED	4	36	26 NO RE-USE OF SINGLE SERVICE ARTICLES	2	55	**LIGHTING**		
08 FOOD PROTECTION DURING STORAGE, PREPARATION, DISPLAY, SERVICE, TRANSPORTATION	2	37	**WATER**			38 LIGHTING PROVIDED AS REQUIRED, FIXTURES SHIELDED	1	67
09 HANDLING OF FOOD (ICE) MINIMIZED	2	38	*27 WATER SOURCE, SAFE HOT AND COLD UNDER PRESSURE	5	56	**VENTILATION**		
10 IN USE, FOOD (ICE) DISPENSING UTENSILS PROPERLY STORED	1	39	**SEWAGE**			39 ROOMS AND EQUIPMENT VENTED AS REQUIRED	1	68
PERSONNEL			*28 SEWAGE AND WASTE WATER DISPOSAL	4	57	**DRESSING ROOMS**		
*11 PERSONNEL WITH INFECTIONS RESTRICTED	5	40	**PLUMBING**			40 ROOMS CLEAN, LOCKERS PROVIDED, FACILITIES CLEAN, LOCATED, USED	1	69
*12 HANDS WASHED AND CLEAN, GOOD HYGIENIC PRACTICES	5	41	29 INSTALLED, MAINTAINED	1	58	**OTHER OPERATIONS**		
13 CLEAN CLOTHES, HAIR RESTRAINTS	1	42	*30 CROSS-CONNECTION, BACK SIPHONAGE, BACKFLOW	5	59	*41 NECESSARY TOXIC ITEMS PROPERLY STORED, LABELED, USED	5	70
FOOD EQUIPMENT AND UTENSILS			**TOILET AND HANDWASHING FACILITIES**			42 PREMISES MAINTAINED, FREE OF LITTER UNNECESSARY ARTICLES, CLEANING MAINTENANCE EQUIPMENT PROPERLY STORED, AUTHORIZED PERSONNEL	1	71
14 FOOD (ICE) CONTACT SURFACES DESIGNED, CONSTRUCTED, MAINTAINED, INSTALLED, LOCATED	2	43	*31 NUMBER, CONVENIENT, ACCESSIBLE DESIGNED, INSTALLED	4	60	43 COMPLETE SEPARATION FROM LIVING/SLEEPING QUARTERS, LAUNDRY	1	72
15 NON-FOOD CONTACT SURFACES DESIGNED, CONSTRUCTED, MAINTAINED, INSTALLED, LOCATED	1	44	32 TOILET ROOMS ENCLOSED, SELF CLOSING DOORS, FIXTURES, GOOD REPAIR, CLEAN, HAND CLEANSER, SANITARY TOWELS/TISSUE/HAND-DRYING DEVICES PROVIDED, PROPER WASTE RECEPTACLES	2	61	44 CLEAN, SOILED LINEN PROPERLY STORED	1	73
16 DISHWASHING FACILITIES, DESIGNED, CONSTRUCTED, MAINTAINED, INSTALLED, LOCATED, OPERATED	2	45						
17 ACCURATE THERMOMETERS, CHEMICAL TEST KITS PROVIDED, GAUGE COCK (¼ IPS VALVE)	1	46	**FOLLOW-UP** YES 1 / NO 2		74	**RATING SCORE** (100 - Less Weight of Items Violated)	75 76 77	

* CRITICAL ITEMS REQUIRING IMMEDIATE ACTION

RECEIVED BY (Name and Title)

INSPECTED BY (Name and Number and Title)

FORM FD 2420 (5/78) PREVIOUS EDITIONS ARE OBSOLETE   Use reverse for remarks (80-1)

For sale by the Supt. of Documents, U.S. Government Printing Office, Wash., D.C. 20402 (Per 50 copies)

Stock No. 017-012-00264-1

FIG. 7.1. Foodservice establishment inspection form available from Food and Drug Administration, Washington DC.

operations is evident by examining a U.S. Public Service inspection form that is used by many health departments (Fig. 7.1). Inspections are made periodically to determine if the foodservice operation is following procedures which insure that food is prepared in a sanitary and safe manner. Item numbers 02 and 08 on this inspection report are concerned with keeping the food itself clean. The cleanliness of the workers' clothes is addressed in number 13. Numbers 15 and 23 deal with the cleanliness of surfaces and equipment that do not even come into contact with the food. Even such areas as plumbing and sewage (numbers 28–30), toilet facilities (31 and 32), garbage areas (33 and 34), walls and floors (36 and 37), lights (38), ventilation (39), dressing rooms (40) and laundry (43 and 44) are considered important enough to be inspected by health officials. These items are not concerned with sanitation per se but rather the cleanliness of the foodservice area.

SANITATION

All sanitation programs should start with good housekeeping practices. Once the area is clean (free of dirt and litter) the second step is to insure that food contact surfaces are sanitized.

Items may be sanitized in one of two ways: (1) by the use of high temperatures or (2) by the use of special chemicals. Either method will kill bacteria and thus sanitize the particular item.

Once again the areas of importance are identified by studying the inspection form in Fig. 7.1. Number 17 refers to the temperature or the use of bacteria-killing chemicals in the dish machine, while numbers 19 and 20 address the temperature and chemical concentrations necessary for sanitizing of equipment that is washed by hand.

Local, state and federal governments publish vast amounts of information that are helpful in training personnel in the areas of sanitation. Contact your local health department for useful pamphlets and audiovisual training tools to help in this important area of foodservice.

FOOD POISONING

Most food poisoning occurs because of bacterial contamination of the food. The most common sources of the bacteria are food and people. For example, poultry has lots of bacteria on the skin and inside the cavity. Hair, hands, scratches or wounds and the mouth by sneezes and coughs are all sources of bacteria from people. Although the actual type of bacteria may vary, the food poisoning symptoms and reasons for the contamination are similar. All bacteria must have food, moisture and the proper temperature to survive. Sanitizing procedures are designed to deprive the bacteria of one or more of these conditions so that either the organisms will die or at least not multiply.

As noted earlier items in the kitchen that come into contact with food are sanitized either by using high temperatures or chemicals. After the food contact surfaces have been sanitized, the next step in preventing food poisoning is to be sure the food is handled properly.

FOOD HANDLING

The food must be from a reliable source and arrive at the facility in good condition. Health departments require that food be stored properly. These items are numbers 01 and 02 in the inspection report (Fig. 7.1).

Next comes the important task of preparing the food in a manner that will prevent bacterial contamination. First, of course, the food must be prevented from getting dirty. This is covered in number 08 in the inspection report. A major source of contamination is the employee with dirty hands, dirty hair, scratches or wounds and airborne germs from coughs or sneezes. Prevention of the spread of bacteria from foodservice workers is covered in numbers 11, 12 and 13 in the form in Fig. 7.1.

Bacteria grows best between the temperatures of 60° and 120°F. This range of temperatures is called the danger zone and is demonstrated on a thermometer schematic in Fig. 7.2. The foodservice supervisor should aim to keep foods above 120°F or below 60°F as much of the time as possible so that bacterial growth is kept at a minimum. Several checks on the temperatures of food are made by the inspector (note numbers 03, 04, 05 and 06 in Fig. 7.1). The adage "Keep hot foods hot and keep cold foods cold" is important not only for customer satisfaction, but for the prevention of food poisoning.

The precautions for sanitation and food handling must be carefully followed. The astute manager will devise check lists, cleaning schedules, and temperature control procedures to assure that the staff is following correct procedures for a safe and clean foodservice operation. Inspections will be made routinely (see Fig. 7.3).

Food Poisoning Outbreak

One problem college and university foodservices face can be state and national notoriety. If a commercial restaurant gives food poisoning to 10 or 20 people, the customers affected go their separate ways and have "the flu." Some might suspect food poisoning, but due to the scattering of the restaurant customers throughout the city they have trouble confirming their suspicions.

On the other hand, think what would happen to a college if there were an outbreak of food poisoning. When students come down with the flu, they think, and the school paper prints it as fact, that food poisoning has taken place.

Once the article is printed the damage is done. No matter how hard the school tries, the stigma remains. State and national press will jump on a suspected foodborne illness problem at any of our major colleges or universities.

A local restaurant does not have the media appeal as does a college, with its alumni, students, parents and relatives scattered throughout a state or the country. In a local restaurant, food poisoning is interpreted as the flu and in a college setting flu is interpreted as food poisoning.

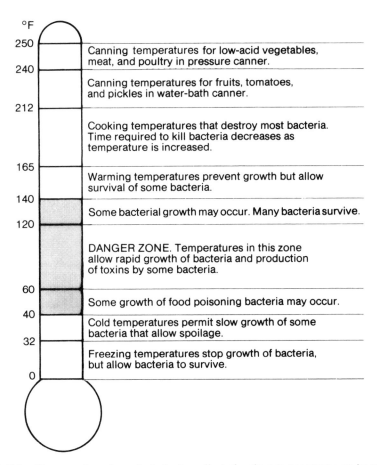

FIG. 7.2. Thermometer schematic indicating effect of various temperatures on bacteria.

Based on an inspection this day, the items marked below are violations of Act 368 P.A. 1978 in operation or facilities which must be corrected by the next routine inspection, or within a period specified by the Health Authority in writing. Failure to comply with this notice may result in license suspension and/or other legal action. You have the right to appeal any violations listed.

OWNER OR OPERATOR

FOOD AND BEVERAGE VENDING MACHINE INSPECTION REPORT

Time　　　　Date

Health Department

VENDOR NAME

ADDRESS

CITY OR TOWNSHIP

ZIP CODE

LOCATION OF MACHINE(S)　　　　ZIP CODE

TYPE OF MACHINE　1. MILK　2. SANDWICH　3. ICE CREAM　4 SOFT DRINK (Post Mix)
5 SOFT DRINK (Pre Mix)　6 SOFT DRINK (Packaged)　7. NON-POTENTIALLY HAZARDOUS FOOD　8. COFFEE　9. OTHER

COMPANY NAME, ADDRESS AND TELEPHONE NUMBER POSTED　☐ YES　☐ NO

ITEM

MACHINE VIOLATIONS
01 Food Source, Sound
02 Original Container, Properly Labeled
03 Food Protection During Loading, Storage, Display, Vending
04 Facilities To Maintain Product Temperature
05 Safety Controls
06 Thermometers
07 Food Contact Surfaces Potentially Hazardous Food, Cleaned, Rinsed, Sanitized, Frequency
08 Food Contact Surfaces Designed, Constructed, Safe Materials, Accessible, Good Repair
09 Interior Non-Food Contact Surfaces Designed, Constructed, Clean, Accessible, Good Repair

ITEM

10 Draining, Diversion Devices, Retention Pans
11 Plumbing Air Gap, Toxic Materials, Filters, Valves, Backflow, Screens
12 Exterior Surfaces Designed, Constructed, Maintained, Clean
13 Insect and Rodent Proof Doors, Screens, Covers, Service Connections
14 Easily Moveable, Elevated, Kickplates, Sealed

EMPLOYEE VIOLATIONS
15 Personnel With Infections Restricted
16 Cleanliness, Good Hygienic Practices, Hands Washed and Clean

AREA VIOLATIONS
17 Food Protection During Storage, Transportation

ITEM

18 Safe Temperatures, Product
19 Condiments Protected, Dispensed, Dispenser Cleaned, Rinsed and Sanitized
20 Lighted, Ventilated, No Leakage or Condensation
21 Floors Constructed, Clean, Harborage
22 Handwashing Facilities Hot/Cold Water, Soap, Towels, Convenient, Available
23 Single-Service Articles Storage, Dispensing, Protection
24 Microwave Ovens and Other Equipment Cleaned, Rinsed, Sanitized, Frequency, In Compliance
25 Cleaning Record
26 Water Source Safe, Pressure
27 Plumbing Installed, Maintained, Cross-Connection, Backflow
28 Waste Receptacles Construction, Frequency, Clean, Located

MACHINE MODEL NO. & SERIAL NO.	TYPE	INSP.	ITEMS VIOLATED	COMMENT
1.				
2.				
3.				
4.				
5.				
6.				
7.				

RECEIVED BY　　INSPECTED BY　　FOLLOW-UP Yes . . . . No . . . .

USE REVERSE FOR REMARKS　　By Authority of Act 368, P.A. 1978, as amended

FIG. 7.3.　Food and beverage vending machine inspection report.

FOOD POISONING INVESTIGATION

The first thing to do when food poisoning is suspected is to try and determine which meal was the probable cause. Leftovers from that meal should be stored in an area that is secure to prevent them from being served or discarded until the investigation is complete.

Each school, based on local or state requirements, has its own procedure for handling suspected food-borne illness cases. Be familiar with your school's procedures in advance.

A written procedure should be available in each unit serving food. Questions that need answering are the following:

1. Who needs to be notified if a food-borne illness is suspected?
2. Where are patients sent for help and testing?
3. Who conducts the investigation, by (a) interviewing the customers, (b) examining the suspected food items, (c) quarantining the suspected food and (d) testing the food samples?
4. Who releases information to the press and public?
5. How are public relations handled?

Food items that were served during the suspected meal should not be offered again to the customers.

An interview with those who are sick, and those who think they are, is one of the first steps. The interview questions should be as follows.

1. Where did you eat during the last 3 days?
2. What foods did you eat at those locations?
3. Did any of the food items taste funny?
4. Who did you eat with?
5. What did they have to eat?
6. Did you eat this food right away or did it sit around for awhile?
7. When did you start to feel sick?
8. What are your symptoms?

The only way you can be positive that your operation did not cause food poisoning is if none of the sick people ate in the school dining room during the period in question.

The interview is used to identify the suspected meal and menu items. The time between eating and the onset of symptoms is also a factor. Some types of poisoning show symptoms early (between 2 and 6 hours) and others do not show until much later (up to 30 days).

If the 10 sick people interviewed all had chicken for lunch yesterday, and 10 orders of chicken were sold, then it looks as if food poisoning is the cause of the illness. On the other hand, if the 10 sick people had 10 different foods and six portions of each item were sold, it is more difficult to blame the illness on contaminated food.

The interviewers are looking for a link between some or all of the sick people and a common food. For example, there are 100 sick people in the building. It could be that 80 have the flu and 20 have food poisoning. The thing to remember is that just because you find a number of students that have the flu does not mean that some of the group does not have food poisoning.

The local health department will assist in the investigation and probably test the food and stool samples.

A food-borne illness can be devastating to any foodservice, in particular to a college or university. Even though students may not remember some school incidents, they will be sure to hand the information about food poisoning at school down through the years.

REFERENCES

AVERY, A.C. 1980. A Modern Guide to Foodservice Equipment. CBI Publishing Co., Boston, MA.

CICHY, R. F. 1981. The application of quality assurance principles to a commissary foodservice system. Ph.D. Thesis, Dept. of Food Service and Human Nutrition. Michigan State University, East Lansing, MI.

FIELDS, M. L. 1979. Fundamentals of Food Microbiology. AVI Publishing Co., Westport, CT.

GRAHAM, H. D. 1980. Safety of Foods. AVI Publishing Co., Westport, CT.

GUTHRIE, R. K. 1980. Food Sanitation, 2nd Edition. AVI Publishing Co., Westport, CT.

MICHIGAN'S FOOD SERVICE SANITATION STATUTE. 1978. Public Health Code, Act 368, Part 129, as amended. Lansing, MI.

MINOR, L. J. 1983. Sanitation, Safety and Environmental Standards. AVI Publishing Co., Westport, CT.

NIFI. 1974. Applied Foodservice Sanitation: A Certification Coursebook. National Institute for the Foodservice Industry, 120 S. Riverside Plaza, Chicago, IL.

NRA. (n.d.) Food-Borne Illnesses (Reference Chart). National Restaurant Association, Chicago, IL.

NRA. (n.d.) Pest Prevention. National Restaurant Association, Chicago, IL.

NSF. 1976, Standards on Food Service Equipment. National Sanitation Foundation, Ann Arbor, MI.

SHORT, J. M. (editor). 1966. Recommended methods for the Microbiological Examination of Foods. 2nd Edition. American Public Health Association, New York, NY.

USDHHS. 1962. Food Service Sanitation Manual, Pub. no. 934, U.S. Dept. of Health and Human Services, Washington, DC.

8 Food Vending

The general purpose of vending is to provide the campus community with 24-hour-a-day services in these four basic categories: (1) food, (2) amusement games, (3) laundry and (4) miscellaneous (cigarettes, newspapers, stamps and sundry items). Food vending can be broken down into the following groups: (1) cold beverages, (2) hot beverages, (3) candy and chips, (4) cold food, (5) hot food, (6) ice cream, (7) milk and juice and (8) pastry. The food vended on each campus depends on how available these items are from cafeterias and snack shops, for faculty, staff, students and guests.

For example, on a campus of 1,000 students in the middle of a business community with five or six fast-food restaurants and convenience stores surrounding the school there would not be much need for food vending machines. On the other hand if this school has a lot of night classes and the local fast-food restaurants and convenience stores are fancy restaurants or are not open at night, there could be a need for vending.

The first question to ask is whether or not there is a need for vending machines. If the answer is yes, then a decision has to be made as to what products and/or services should be offered. Next comes the choice between owning the machines or contracting with a commercial vendor who will in most cases pay the school a commission.

There are pros and cons for either running your own service or contracting it out to private enterprise. Some schools feel they can make more money and have better control by operating their own service. Others think that large companies such as A.R.A., Canteen, or Servomation or even medium-sized local firms can do a better job than the school can.

Each school has to look at and evaluate its own situation. Are good employees available? Are the school employees unionized? Is there adequate storage space? Are enough machines involved to warrant going into the business?

OUTSIDE VENDORS

This chapter will deal with the assumption that the school does not want to run a vending business but chooses to contract with an outside firm.

By issuing the contract to a private company, problems do not disappear, they are just different. The main problems deal with trying to control details through an owner–contractor relationship. The school and the vending company do not always agree on what is the best way to run the operation. It is similar in nature to trying to run a company through absentee ownership. It is as if the manager is looking through a plate glass window—he or she can see but cannot touch.

Commissions

Some schools choose not to receive a commission, but just offer vending services to the school community. Others, especially in these times of tight funds, decide to use a combination, offering the services at a fair price and receiving part of the profits in the form of a commission from the vendor.

Comparing one school's commission rate to another is like trying to compare food costs. A comparison cannot be made until all the facts are known. Questions to be answered include: How many machines are there? What is the selling price of the items? How much are total sales? What are the costs? Who pays for electricity and water? Are the machines located near each other? Is parking for service and repair personnel close to each stop? Is each location just inside the door or up three sets of stairs without an elevator? Is the vendor required to put in new machines? Is the vendor's warehouse close by or does the vendor have to travel 60 miles to get there? Who pays taxes? Are there parking permits to buy? How about vandalism and theft—who pays? or is it shared? Was there strong competition or just one company giving a quote? How many days each week is service required? Are repairs required on nights or on weekends?

If two schools have the same answers to that list of questions, then each should be getting the same commission. Otherwise commissions will vary. The rates are determined in a variety of ways. Some contracts specify one commission percentage rate for all products vended (single rate system). Other contracts set the rate differently for each category of products (variable rate system). Yet another method is to have a certain level of sales before the commissions are paid to the school. Then as sales increase so does the percentage commission (increasing rate system). These three systems are illustrated in Table 8.1.

TABLE 8.1. Commission Rates by Systems

| | Single rate (%) | Variable rates (%) | Increasing rates | |
			Sales per month	(%)
Candy	18	22	$0 to under $ 1,000	0
			$ 1,000 to under $ 2,000	5
			$ 2,000 to under $ 2,500	15
			$ 2,500 up	25
Beverage, cold	18	20	$0 to under $ 1,500	0
			$ 1,500 to under $ 4,000	8
			$ 4,000 to under $ 6,000	15
			$ 6,000 to under $ 8,000	22
			$ 8,000 to under $10,000	24
			$10,000 up	26
Ice cream	18	12	$0 to under $ 3,000	0
			$ 3,000 to under $ 5,000	5
			$ 5,000 up	13

The increasing rate system can be established for any length of time—a month, semester, quarter, 6 months, or a year.

There are two methods of interpreting the increasing rate system of calculating commissions—one is a straight sales formula and the other is a retroactive formula. Assume the two formulas would result in different commissions being paid to the school. For example, assume cold beverage sales for the semester is $6200. The commissions paid to the school under the *straight sales formula* would be calculated as follows:

```
    0% paid on sales up to $1,500           1500 =    $0
    8% paid on the next $2500 sales   (1500–4000) =   200
   15% paid on the next $2000 sales   (4000–6000) =   300
   22% paid on the next $200 sales    (6000–6200) =    44
         Total commission paid on $6200 sales        $544
```

Using the *retroactive formula* the total sales are added up and the commission percentage at that level is paid on all sales. Using the $6200 cold beverage sales as our example, the formula in Table 8.1 specifies 22% sales between $6000 to under $8000. The commission paid, using a retroactive formula, would then be 0.22×6200 or $1364. That is a difference of $820 using the same percentage figures but calculating the commission by different methods. This is an excellent example of why it is important to make sure that the contract is not ambiguous.

Another ambiguous area in contracts is not closing the gap on income brackets. This leaves a few pennies (in some cases) or a dollar (in other cases) between categories and allows an area, even though very small, open to interpretation.

The problem with setting up a commission based on the following scale is the area of confusion at each level ($1500, $4000, $6000, $8000 and $10000). What commission is paid when sales exactly hit one of those figures?

```
Beverage, cold
      $0 through $  1500     0%
$  1500 through $  4000     8%
$  4000 through $  6000    15%
$  6000 through $  8000    22%
$  8000 through $10000    24%
$10000 up                 26%
```

The likelihood of this happening is rare, but why should it be left open to interpretation? Assume that sales for the month are not $6200 as in the previous example, but exactly $6000.

You are in charge of the vending contract and you tell your boss that the check will be for $1320 (22% × $6000 sales as stipulated in the scale). Two weeks later the vendor walks in with a check made out to the school for $900 (15% × $6000 sales). Who is right? Should the check be $900 or $1320? Either could be right because the $6000 figures appear in both the 15% and the 22% lines. Since the vendor's formula, not the school's, is on the bid, it would probably hold up in court that the $900 figure is right. Try explaining the $420 shortage to your boss.

If you had used the wording "4000 to under $6000" it becomes clear that the check would have to be for $1320.

Some contracts try to avoid this problem by narrowing the gap.

```
  $0–$1499     0%
$1500–$3999     8%
$4000–$5999    15%
$6000–$7999    22%
```

Again there is an area, ever so small but still there, of the $1.00 between categories. Unless all items are sold in $1.00 increments you could have sales of $3999.50, $3999.75, or sales of $5999.95. Which commission rate is going to be paid? The school would want the higher rate and the vendor would want to pay the lower.

If the gap is narrowed to the smallest denominator of sales, probably a nickel, the wording *through* or *to* can be used without causing a problem. Just to be sure, go as low as a penny. It works, but is cumbersome with all those nines:

```
  $0–$1499.99     0%
$1500–$3999.99     8%
$4000–$5999.99    15%
$6000–$7999.99    22%
```

A solution is to use the wording *to under* as was done in Table 8.1.

Bidding

The objectives of bidding any contract are to allow qualified companies an opportunity to obtain the business and at the same time get the best deal possible for the school.

The manager responsible for vending could telephone three or four companies in the area and ask them to submit proposals. The proposals received would have as many different specifications as there are companies. It may be very difficult to judge one proposal against another to decide which would be the best. Therefore, it becomes obvious that the manager should establish the terms of the contract and set up the specifications for companies to bid on.

The two main reasons for setting up bid specifications are (1) to make sure that the school will get exactly what it needs and (2) to make sure that all companies are bidding on the same thing.

The bid can be either an open or a sealed bid. The difference is that a sealed bid cannot be inspected until a specified date and time. As bids are received by the school they are left unopened until that time. This prevents the possibility of bidding companies finding out in advance what their competition is offering.

An open bid could be either the school conducting an auction, or by the manager privately reading the bids as they arrive. In auction bidding, all interested parties are invited to meet in a certain place at a specified time. The procedure would go something like this:

The director of vending starts the auction by asking for a bid. One vendor may offer 10%. Another may say 10.5%. The third may increase it to 11%. Vendor number two counters with 11.5%, and the bidding continues until no one is willing to go any higher. At this point whoever was the last (highest) bidder receives the contract award.

The disadvantage to the school in this type of bidding is that there could be a loss of income to the school. As an example, on a closed bid, Company A, the high bidder, might offer 20%, with Company B at 15%, and Company C at 14%. If, in this example, the Director of Vending had conducted an auction bid instead of a closed bid, Company C would have dropped out of the competition at 14% and Company B at 15%. That would mean the top bidder, Company A, could stop bidding at 15.5% or maybe 15.25%. True the second and third place bidders might go over their original bids, but probably not up to the 20% level that the school received under the closed bid.

In the other type of open bidding, the manager unseals and inspects the bids as they arrive in the office. Bid closing time and dates are still specified but prior inspection by the manager can take place.

A SAMPLE CONTRACT

This section will review a bid paragraph by paragraph. After each section an explanation will follow explaining what it means and why it is necessary. Remember that the idea is to make sure that the bid is written so that it cannot be interpreted more than one way. Since this bid specification will become the contract, everything has to be written clearly so no misunderstanding can occur.

American Booklearning College

February 3, 1986

Food Vending Bid

Bids must be submitted on this form and in accordance with all conditions listed hereon. Bids and amendments thereto, or withdrawals of bids, must be received in writing by the Director of Vending prior to the date and time specified for the public bid opening: 3:30 P.M., Thursday, March 6, 1986.

The heading of this sample contract states what the bid is and who it is for. In this case the bid is for ABC College, and it is the bid for food vending, not for video games or laundry machines.

February 3 is the day the bids were mailed and each company has until 3:30 P.M. on March 6 (about 4 weeks after receipt) to inspect, calculate and submit their bids.

The person receiving the bid is listed and a statement that unless it is in writing and received *prior* to the bid opening it will not be considered.

A public bid opening means that anyone wishing to be present can attend and watch and listen to the offers made by each company.

American Booklearning College as applied in this contract, shall hereafter be referred to as ABC.

In the interest of brevity there is no sense in always writing out American Booklearning College. A statement should be made as to what the initials stand for.

This is a sealed bid. Please submit your bid in a sealed envelope, clearly marked *Bid for Food Vending Machines* with the name of your company on the back of the mailing envelope. Submit your bid to

> Mr. Walter Thompson, Director of Vending
> American Booklearning College
> Address
> City, State, Zip

This is a sealed bid, with each company submitting its bid in an envelope that will not be opened until the date and time stipulated. Some schools enclose a special return envelope that is color coded or prominently marked "BID" to prevent it being opened prior to the date and time. It can be very embarrassing if the envelope is mistakenly opened early. It could even lead to a lawsuit.

The specification states who is authorized to receive the bid with title and address for mailing.

The name of the bidder is requested on the envelope to allow the school to keep track of which bids have been received. If the college knows that a particular company was planning on bidding and its bid has not been received by the last incoming mail, the company can be contacted. This will also allow the school to answer a company's question as to whether or not its bid has been received.

> Each supplier is responsible for bid delivery to the Director of Vending. ABC cannot be held responsible for any bid received after the bid opening. No oral modifications will be considered. Bids received after 3:29 P.M., Thursday, March 6, 1986 will not be considered, and will be returned to the bidder, unopened.

The last word in this paragraph indicates that it is important not to mistakenly open the bid. Suppose that XYZ Company's bid is received in the mail a day late, opened by someone in the office and its bid is high. (Remember that in this type of bidding the highest bid is the best and gets the contract.) How do you tell XYZ that they sent their bid in late and therefore are disqualified? They could claim a violation of the contract since their bid was opened, and therefore all bids should be rejected. They might protest that the Director of Vending received the bid on time and was in collusion with the next bidder. A possibility of a lawsuit exists.

The contract puts the responsibility for getting the bid to the Director of Vending on the supplier. Without this paragraph suppliers could say delivery was out of their control, because of poor mail service or any number of reasons. If the contract is large enough, or the supplier is local, a company representative might hand carry the bid to the Director of Vending.

"No oral modification will be considered." This prevents losing bidders from saying they offered something verbally on the phone or in a conversation and that they should receive the contract award. This indicates to the bidders that if it is not in writing it will not be considered.

> The Director of Vending reserves the right to reject any or all bids, or to accept any bid which, in the opinion of ABC officials, will better serve the University. Attach a letter outlining, by section, any conditions your firm cannot meet and your alternate proposals for those conditions.

The first sentence is an escape clause and at the same time gives the flexibility to accept alternate bids. In some cases the alternate proposal might be better than the one specified. Without this clause in the contract, the alternate would have to be thrown out.

The second sentence requires the bidder to outline conditions that cannot be met. They will be less able to hide the fact that they cannot meet the specifications. This avoids unpleasant discoveries later in the contract year.

> One total contract shall be awarded to one supplier for the period specified. It is the intent of ABC to award this contract to the supplier meeting all 38 general conditions and offering the highest bid, based on the Grand Total Commission of anticipated sales.

One total contract means that the vending concessions will not be split giving the cold beverage concession to one company and candy to another. Note that your school may want to do the opposite and split the contract.

If there were only six machines on campus (two soft-drink, two candy and two pastry), it would be difficult to get three different companies to come in because it would not be profitable. On the other hand one company could send in one truck and one driver to take care of all the machines, making this a profitable account. An operation requiring 100 machines (50 soft-drink and 50 candy) may actually work better with two different companies, one soft-drink company and one candy company.

The second sentence establishes the grounds you are going to use to award the contract. The Grand Total Commission will be covered at the end of this section.

Through this point in the contract the rules for the bidding have been set up. The remainder of the contract deals with the specific conditions that each bidder must meet.

Award and Contract Subject to These 38 General Conditions

1. EFFECTIVE DATE OF THIS CONTRACT: July 1, 1986 for a period of five (5) years, expiring on June 30, 1991.

The heading states that there are 38 conditions that must be met before the contract will be awarded.

Condition 1 specifies the length of the contract and when it starts. It would not seem necessary to give the expiration date as anyone should be able to add 5 years or 3 years to an existing figure. But to be thorough and prevent any confusion list all three: the starting date, the length and the ending date.

Many contracts have numbers in both written and numerical form, e.g., five (5), eight (8), two (2). This is done to minimize mistakes by someone reading the document in a hurry.

   2.   THE DIRECTOR OF VENDING will be the administrator and ABC's representative for the duration of this contract. The vendor will assign a management staff member as its representative to ABC. This staff member will report to the Director of Vending for all terms of this contract.

This condition establishes the two people responsible for the administration of the contract. The vendor knows whom to contact and who is the voice of the school. This section is probably more important to the vendor than the school.

The school may have a number of vice presidents. It may also have a number of buildings that are run by either department heads or deans. As a protection for the vendor, there is one person—one control point or place of authority—for the vendor to work with. This person acts as the school's voice. Deans and department heads should work through this person to the vendor. If the vendor receives requests or commands from anyone else, the Director of Vending must approve them.

   3.   The Vendor receiving the bid must be an equal opportunity employer and have an affirmative action program. Attach a letter attesting to both. Failure to comply during the life of the contract will be grounds for cancellation.
                         Page 1 of 10 pages

A letter is requested because some large companies may have a very long document describing the affirmative action program. There is no need to have a detailed copy; all that is necessary is a statement that the company does have an affirmative action program.

Each page of the contract should be numbered as a check that no pages are missing.

On some contracts there is a place for the bidder to initial each page that is returned with the bid. This is done to prevent the accusation by a bidder that conditions were changed and a new page (unseen by the bidder) was inserted with different information.

4. Each supplier must bid on, and be able to supply, all machines and products outlined in this contract.

For example, the contract designates 21 machines (10 candy, 10 cold beverage and one ice cream). The ice cream machine is important to the school. Without this condition listed in the contract, the high bidder could be a company that does not handle ice cream machines and bids on candy and cold beverages. With this condition in the bid, the company without the ice cream could submit an alternate bid. The school could reject the alternate bid, or it could accept it and eliminate the ice cream machine.

5. This contract or any part thereof cannot be assigned, transferred, or subcontracted to another company, or individual, without full written consent and approval of the Director of Vending.

The concern here is for the school to know what is going on and to have the option of accepting or rejecting the subcontractor.

Is the subcontractor a reliable firm? Are its facilities clean and its trucks in good condition? This gives the school the opportunity to review, and to approve or reject the subcontracted company.

Note that the approval has to be in writing. If the term *written* was not included in the contract the vendor could say a verbal agreement had been made. The written consent is from the director of vending at the school, not from the vendor. If the contract had said written *request* the vendor could have a copy in the company files and never have sent it to the school.

Subcontracting in itself is not necessarily bad. Going back to the contract with 21 machines and only one dispensing ice cream, it might be best for all concerned if the ice cream machine is subcontracted to another company. By having this condition it puts control of the contract where it should be—in the hands of the manager of the school.

6. The Vendor guarantees to protect ABC, its agent or employees from liability of any nature or kind in connection with this contract by either acts or omissions. The Vendor will furnish adequate protection from damages to ABC property and will repair damages of any kind for which the Vendor, its suppliers, or its employees are responsible.

This is an example of a *hold harmless* clause. The first sentence protects the school by either acts (driver runs into another vehicle) or omissions (does not provide adequate electrical grounding of equipment). The last sentence talks about school property and says that it will be repaired by the vendor if the damage is caused by the company or its suppliers. This puts the responsibility on the vendor. The vendor cannot say that a problem was his supplier's fault and have the school deal directly with that firm. It becomes the vendor's responsibility to deal with its suppliers and employees.

7. The Vendor shall carry insurance with companies authorized to do business in Michigan and acceptable to ABC. The policy shall remain in force for the duration of the contract and shall provide coverage as follows:

   A. Worker's compensation   Statutory
       Employer's liability $100,000
   B. Comprehensive general liability
      1. Bodily injury   Each occurrence
      2. Property damage Each occurrence
   C. Comprehensive automotive liability
      1. Bodily injury   Each person, each occurrence
      2. Property damage Each occurrence
   D. Umbrella liability
      Bodily injury and property damage combined
      Each occurrence

Note: Any combination of primary and umbrella limits in B, C, and D above total $500,000 in each category.

  . The vendor awarded the bid must name ABC as an "Additional Insured" in the Public Liability Insurance policy and submit a copy of all policies to ABC within thirty (30) days of the awarding of the contract.

Check with your school regarding its insurance requirements. Each shool and, more probably, each state, has a standard requirement.

Some schools require all bidders to submit an insurance policy with their bid. This is unnecessary. Why require all bidders to do that work when only one is going to win? The last sentence in this sample requires only the winning bidder to submit copies of policies.

8. Refund Centers: Currently there are ten (10) refund centers on campus with a total of $100. It is the Vendor's responsibility to supply each center with from $2 to $15 of refund money (ABC will specify the amount). The amounts may fluctuate during the life of this contract in order to meet the needs of each location. Every driver shall replenish the refund banks every time a machine is filled. At the discretion of ABC, the number of refund centers may be increased or decreased over the life of this contract.

There are two basic ways of handling refunds for money lost in machines. One is to have a refund center to hand out money at the time of the request; the other is a refund system where the customer requests the money and receives it later. From the customer's standpoint the best system is receiving the money immediately.

In the past when soft drinks were 25¢ and candy 15¢, customers were less apt to make false claims for refunds. At today's prices, refund centers are more vulnerable to false requests. For example, it is an easy way to make money claiming a refund when cigarettes are selling for over a dollar a pack.

A log can be kept by a receptionist or office worker in either method of refunds. With the availability and easy use of computers each person's name can be recorded, listing the date, type of produce and the amount of the refund. Just the fact that the name is being recorded will have a tendency to keep people honest.

The computer can help the manager perform a number of tasks for the operation:

a.   List the customers' names and the number of times each receives a refund over a specified period of time.

b.   Show which type of vending (candy machines, cigarettes, milk) results in the most refunds.

c.   List repair records for individual machines to indicate when they should be replaced.

d.   Compare sales to the number of repairs on each machine (Table 8.2). These records can be used to identify which manfacturer's machines are the most reliable. Without computers, normally these records are not maintained and the school has only a guess of which machines need replacing. It can be seen in Table 8.2 that although the machine in Building A had more than twice the number of repairs, the sales per repair were still more than twice that in Building B. The machine in Building A is actually performing better than the one in Building B. Decisions for replacement of machines can now be based on actual performance rather than guesswork.

e.   Total the sales from the vending machines, subtract the refunds and compare that to expected sales from the products vended. This should balance. If there are machines that do not balance then a review of the repair and refund records should be made. A check on the machines to see if they are operating properly should also be made. Inventory control is easier and it will tell you if customers are asking for undeserved refunds.

TABLE 8.2.   Year-to-Date Repairs vs. Sales

	Machines			Refunds ($)	Sales		Repairs		Sales per repair	
I.D. no.	Manufacturer	Location	Type		Month ($)	Year ($)	Month (no.)	Year (no.)	Month ($)	Year ($)
CA 345	Francis	Building A	Candy			7000		12		580
CA 401	Lopes	Building B	Candy			1000		5		200

9. The Vendor shall secure and pay for all permits, governmental fees, and licenses. It shall pay all federal, state and local taxes and assessments which may be levied against its equipment or merchandise while in or upon the premises of ABC. This is to include any fines which may be levied in connection with the operation of the Vendor's business upon the premises of ABC.

The bid specifies who is accountable for the fees and taxes. You could stipulate that the school will pay all fees or maybe some are paid by you and some by the vendor. In any case it should be clear who is responsible.

10. Commissions to ABC will be computed on gross sales. All commissions shall be paid by check, payable to ABC University, and delivered to the Director of Vending not later than the 25th of the following month. Computer printouts (two copies) listing machine numbers, locations and sales with the amount of commission from each, shall be submitted with each payment. Attach a copy of the type of report that will be used by your company with your bid.

As discussed earlier in the chapter, there are a number of ways to compute commissions. All bidders use the same formula.

The more costs your school assumes—such as paying taxes, absorbing theft (both product and money), paying for repairs of vandalized machines, paying for signs, electricity, water, lights, and area renovations—the higher the commission rate will be from the vendor. The more you require the vendor to do, the lower the commission rate will be. In either case you should make about the same amount of money.

11. The Vendor agrees to keep accurate accounts and records relative to the operation of the vending machines covered by this contract. The Vendor further agrees that such books and records shall be subject to inspection by any person designated by ABC at all reasonable times during business hours.

Is the vendor paying you the right amount of money? Without a lot of trouble, this gives you the right to inspect the vendor's books.

12. Any designee, either an employee or authorized representative of ABC may, unannounced, accompany the Vendor's employees on their campus rounds.

This is another form of audit. It also allows the manager to see how the vendor's employees operate. Is the truck neat and clean? Are the insides of the machines clean? Do they use outdated products? Are refunds handled properly? Do they bang their carts into your doors and walls?

From a money audit standpoint it is a good way to see if all sales are reported. For example—candy sales in F building stay at $15 to $18 a week. The machine is filled on Wednesdays. On a Wednesday you ride with the driver and make a mental note that the machine requires 95 bars to return it to par stock. The manager should ask two questions: (1) Does the report for that week show 95 times $0.30 for a total income of $28.50? and (2) Why were sales so high that one week? Maybe sales are always $28 to $30 and the vendor only reports $15 to $18. This could be the reason this company bid 5% more commission than any other vendor.

13. If a labor dispute between the Vendor and its employees, or a union results in the picketing of, or a work stoppage by any ABC employee, ABC may immediately cancel this contract.

Read this one carefully. It does not say that the vendor's employees cannot go on strike or picket the vendor. It refers to the response of ABC's employees to the vendor's labor dispute. You do not want your school to go on strike because the vendor's employees are picketing the campus.

14. Either party may cancel this contract with ninety (90) days prior written notice.

The cancellation from the standpoint of either party should be justified and for good cause. Remember the vendor has spent a lot of time and money in setting up this account.

The 90 days gives both parties time to plan the next step. It gives the school enough time to contact the second best bidder or even to rebid the contract.

15. The Vendor shall furnish machines in all present locations on campus, and in any new locations designated by ABC, in existing buildings, or in new buildings as completed. All machines and locations shall be identified by corresponding numbers. The Vendor shall not transfer any machine to another location without written approval of the Director of Vending. New machines must be approved by the Director of Vending. All equipment must present a uniform appearance and be in "like new" condition.

The first sentence informs the bidders that they must have machines in all present locations and that you expect the company to respond to your request for additional machines over the life of the contract. Just so there is no confusion in future years, the words "existing" and "new" are stated.

For accounting purposes, the locations and machines are numbered.

Written approval of the director of vending is required to move machines. The school does not want the vendors to move machines where they want them. If they had their way, all of the machines would be in the middle of every main entrance or lobby, probably blocking traffic.

At the same time, the director of vending acts as the buffer between the vendor, the school employees, students and guests. The company should not get contradictory requests in the placement of the machines.

In "like new" condition is somewhat ambiguous but it is better than nothing and does set some type of expectation.

16. Bidders must inspect the current machine locations prior to submitting bids. Contact Mr. Thompson, Director of Vending, for a conducted tour.

In condition 15 we stipulated that the vendor had to put machines in all current locations. Now the contract tells them they must visit those locations.

The tour should answer these questions:

a. Where should the vendor park its trucks? Are there back docks with easy access to the machines? Are the machines on the first floor, or do vendors have to park their trucks in an area 150 feet from the building? Are there many steps at each entrance? What floors are the machines on, and are there service elevators?

b. Do the trucks and the supervisor's car need a parking permit? If yes, does the permit cost money? Refer to item 9 of the contract to determine who is to pay for the permit. Is there a time limit for parking?

c. What route must the service personnel take to fill the machines? It may be different than the route used to move machines in and out. Are there stairs? Does the service person have to share the elevator with the student body? Is the elevator in good working order? Is the elevator at one end of the building, the machines at the other?

d. Are the electrical outlets close to the machines and is the amperage adequate for the equipment?

e. What kind of space is there for the machines? This vendor may have machines that are a little larger, or all the doors are left hinged. The vendor may have to buy special machines for one or two locations so they can be installed or be filled.

f. Where are the refund centers, next to the machines or up three floors and down two corridors?

g.   Is there a problem of access to any building, or location within a building?

h.   Are there times when machines cannot be serviced because of special situations? For example certain classes are scheduled on Tuesdays and Thursdays and the faculty does not want to be interrupted by the vendor filling machines. Or it could be the opposite—customers want the machine filled by 9 A.M. every day.

17.   Machines required under this contract are as follows:

Machines (no.)	Product	Type
20	Beverage, cold	Standard machines, containing a minimum of 6 selections of 12-oz cans, capacity 288 cans
12	Candy–chips	Glass-front spiral, containing a minimum of 35 selections plus 5 gum and mint (minimum of 40 selections)
8	Candy–chips	Standard machine, containing a minimum of 6 candy, 2 chip and 5 gum and mint (minimum of 13 selections)
12	Cigarettes	Standard machine, containing a minimum of 20 selections
8	Ice cream	Standard machine, containing a minimum of 3 selections
8	Milk–juice	Standard machine, containing a minimum of 6 selections
8	Beverage, hot	Standard machine, containing a minimum of 5 selections: coffee, decaffeinated coffee, soup, hot chocolate and tea
5	Pastry	Standard machine, containing a minimum of 5 selections
5	Food, cold	Standard machine, containing a minimum of 8 selections
2	Food, hot, canned	Standard machine, containing a minimum of 7 selections
5	Microwave ovens	Standard commercial grade machine with push button settings
5	Bill changers	Standard dollar bill changer
2	Condiment stands	As outlined on campus tour
100		

This section makes sure that each vendor bidding on the contract knows how many of each machine are required and what the minimum sizes are.

As an example, this contract requires 12 glass-front spiral candy machines and eight of the old style. The spiral machines cost a lot more to buy. If the amounts were not specified, one bidder could overbid with 20 spirals and another with no spirals.

18.   Each vendor shall supply a list of equipment, with type, manufacturer, model number and illustration, with the bid.

This gives the director of vending an opportunity to verify that the machines are the specified sizes and types.

19.   All machines must be in place and operating within thirty (30) days of the commencing date of this contract, by July 30, 1986.

Without this 30-day clause the company awarded the contract might install half of the machines requested, placing them in the prime locations. After a profit is made, in 6 months or maybe a year, they may use that money to buy machines to be placed in the less profitable locations. Their claim is that they will have the 100 machines in operation by the end of the 5-year contract.

If the total number of machines in the contract is small (10–15), the time period for installation might be about a week. The more machines, the longer the period for installation.

This contract begins during the school's slowest time, allowing for easier movement of machines. It also gives the new vendor's personnel time to get familiar with the campus and their delivery routes.

20. During the life of this contract, requests for additional machines, over and above those listed in condition 17, shall be honored by the Vendor in the quantity specified below:

Beverage, cold	4
Bill changers	1
Candy–chips	4
Cigarettes	2
Food machines, cold	1
Food machines, hot canned	1
Hot beverage	2
Ice cream	2
Microwave oven	1
Milk–juice	1
Pastry	1

The Vendor has sixty (60) days from the time of the written request to have these machines in place and operating. Any requests for machines above these figures will be at the discretion of the Vendor.

This section puts the bidders on notice that the school has the right, under the contract, to request additional machines, and it sets a time limit on the vendor's response to the request.

Trying to anticipate the needs for additional machines over the next 5 years is difficult. The school's building program would influence the number and type of machines listed in this section.

This section also protects the vendor. Once this quantity has been installed the company has the option to turn down requests.

Remember that the vendor is in business to make money. If your additional requests are in prime locations the vendor will, if at all possible, put a machine in.

If additional machines beyond those listed in condition 20 are refused, you can review sales and maybe move a machine from a nonprofitable area to the new area.

21.   The Vendor shall test microwave ovens twice per year, in July and
       December. A written report listing the results and any actions neces-
       sary and/or taken will be submitted to the Director of Vending by
       July 31 and December 31 of each year.

This section defines when microwave ovens are tested and who will test them.
By having the written reports on file you have a backup in case someone questions their safety.

22.   Site locations, and the construction thereof, are the responsibility of
       ABC. ABC shall supply both water and power for the Vendor's use.
       The Vendor is responsible for installing, repairing and maintaining
       each piece of equipment.

This does nothing more than outline who pays for what and who is responsible
for what items.

23.   All machines shall remain the sole property of the Vendor, who shall
       completely maintain them and keep them in constant working order,
       clean and in good appearance. ABC reserves the right to request
       repair, refinishing or replacement of any or all machines. If machines
       are not maintained at the same rate or better than those of the current
       Vendor, it may be grounds for termination of this contract.

This tells who is to maintain the machines. It implies that the school's custo-
dians are not responsible. A sentence could be added stating that the areas around
the machines will be maintained by the school.
    The middle part of this condition gives the school the authority to request
machine replacement. In most instances the vendor will decide on machine
replacement, but on occasions the manager might want to request replacement of
a particular machine.
    The last sentence in the specification is an interesting one. By keeping track of
out-of-order machines and product outages with the old vendor, a school can set
expectations for the new company. As an example, a new vendor gets the
contract. Half way through fall term your office is swamped with complaints that
the machines on campus are always out of order. After analysis, it is discovered
that the machines in the prime locations are in tip-top shape, but those in out-of-
the-way locations are the ones that are always out of order.
    The vendor, to cut setup costs and to get the contract, put good machines in

high volume areas and installed old, cheap machines in out-of-the-way areas; the intent being to repair them if and when they had time.

This last sentence warns the bidders that the manager expects and will be checking to see that all of the machines are working.

24. The Vendor receiving this contract may be asked to install machines to vend items other than those designated in Condition 17, in which case ABC will negotiate the commission rate with the Vendor. The Vendor is required to keep ABC informed on industry trends and innovative ideas.

This contract is for 5 years and the school's needs may change during that period. These changes may be triggered by new inventions (there is now a cotton-candy vending machine) or a change in housing or maybe a request for vending machines with sundry items (combs, toothpaste, nail clippers, etc.).

25. Servicing and repairing of machines must be done seven (7) days per week. Saturday and Sunday servicing is limited to cold beverages and candy–chips in the residence halls plus any out-of-product machines on campus. Repairs must be available seventeen (17) hours per day, from 7:00 A.M. through midnight, seven (7) days per week. Neither service nor repairs are required on ABC's nine (9) recognized holidays. Attach a copy of your organization chart, showing anticipated hours of work per week for employees scheduled to the ABC account.

State what hours you require servicing and repairs. A community college that operates 5 days per week probably would not require the vendor to fill machines on the weekend. A school without students living on campus nor having Sunday classes would not want the vendor to work the staff on Sundays. The added expense would take away from the school's commission and add little in return.

An organization chart listing the employees assigned to the school and their scheduled hours is needed to give you an idea of what kind of service you can expect. As an example: The current vendor has two people spending 40 hours each week filling machines. In addition one service person spends 10 hours each week during the school year. The total is 90 work hours. When bids are opened the highest bidder states that its organization is planning two people, 15 hours each week and a part-time employee 2 hours on Saturday. They say their machines are so good that a maintenance person is not necessary. Their total is 32 hours. This explains why they could offer the best percentage commission and gives the school an indication of what kind of service and repairs to expect.

26. Attach a copy of your preventive maintenance schedule for each type of machine. Show frequencies of mechanical preventive maintenance as well as the schedule and detailed procedures for cleaning.

A fly-by-night company uses verbal communications to describe cleaning procedures. A well-run organization will put it in writing—what cleaning solution to use, how to apply it and how often to clean the machines. The company receiving the contract should have these procedures in writing.

27. The liability for all machines and contents shall remain the sole responsibility of the Vendor. Under no circumstance shall any liabilities whatsoever be accrued against ABC for damage, pilferage, acts of violence, fire or theft, including liability for damages, injury or sickness due to product spoilage or contamination.

This condition puts the total liability on the vendor. Some contracts call for the school to assume some, or maybe all of the liability. The bid and contract should state who is responsible in order for all of the companies to be on an equal bidding basis.

28. Selling prices for the first six (6) months of this contract shall be

	($)
Beverage, cold (12-oz can)	0.60
Beverage, hot	
Coffee (7 oz)	0.30
Hot chocolate (7 oz)	0.30
Soup (7 oz)	0.30
Tea (7 oz)	0.30
Candy	
Bars	0.40
Chips	0.40
Gum	0.40
Mints	0.40
Cigarettes	1.25
Ice cream ($2\frac{1}{2}$-oz bar)	0.40
Milk–juice	
Fruit drinks (8 oz)	0.35
Juice (6 oz)	0.45
Milk (8 oz)	0.40

The school, not the vendor, should set the selling prices. If the prices were not stipulated in the bid, one company may plan on selling all of the above items at $0.05 more than another bidder. It is important that all of the bidding companies use the same selling prices.

The 6-month stipulation keeps the contractor from complaining after the first month that it miscalculated and will have to raise prices to be able to give the school its commission.

29. If after six (6) months it becomes necessary or desirable to change the selling price of products, the commission percentage shall be re-negotiated on those items involved. Pricing will be established by ABC.

After 6 months the vendor will probably make recommendations that can either be approved, modified or rejected.

The director of vending should take product cost changes, vandalism, theft, union contracts and any other increased costs into consideration to establish selling price increases or decreases.

At this time commission rates would also be reviewed. As an example, if the cost of candy increases $0.03 per bar and all other costs remain the same the following are the major options:

1. Keep the selling price the same and reduce commission to the school by $0.03.

2. Raise the selling price $0.05 and split the balance ($0.04 to the vendor and $0.01 to the school).

3. Raise the selling price $0.05 with the school increasing its commission by $0.02.

4. Raise the selling price $0.05 with the vendor keeping it all. If the contract has been in effect for a year or so and the vendor has had a labor contract increase, or gasoline prices have escalated, etc., the school may want to let the vendor recoup some of these expenses by keeping the $0.02.

30. Given the consideration to future trends, sales shall not fall below the patterns established over the last three (3) years.

This condition gives the school a cross-check on how well the vendor keeps the machines repaired and filled, and in general meets the needs of the customers.

Assume that total candy sales have had a steady climb of $500 for the last 3 years. They started at $30,000, moved to $30,500, then $31,000 and—this last year—$31,500. Candy sold for the same prices each year and the student population did not change. Apply the wording of the contract to candy sales at three different hypothetical levels for this year with the new vendor.

A.   Sales are $35,500 (an increase of $4,000 over last year).
B.   Sales are $31,600 (an increase of $100).
C.   Sales are $26,500 (a decrease of $5,000).

Under example A it can be assumed that the new vendor is doing a good job. Sales have increased by more than 12%. Example B is also acceptable, although it is not the $500 per year increase the school had been experiencing. There may have been some problems in the switch over from the previous vendor.

In example C, with sales down almost 16%, there should be some concern with the new vendor. This puts the yellow light on. With conditions about the same (prices the same, people count the same, no drastic change in the economy, no discount candy store opening across the street), the problem has to be the new vendor.

The following questions should be asked:

a.   Are the machines in acceptable working condition or are they out of order all the time?

b.   Are the machines kept stocked or are they empty too often?

c.   Is the product mix acceptable or does the vendor keep unpopular candy bars in the machine?

d.   Is the candy fresh; are the wrappers clean and eye appealing?

e.   Are the machines clean and attractive or do they turn customers away?

31.   Only top of the line, popular brands and products are acceptable. *Prior* to bidding, submit for written approval a complete list outlining by category, brand name and size of *all* items to be supplied and used in your bid. Candy must be from the current top 25 National Candy Buyers Brands Survey. All candy machines must be stocked with _____, _____ and _____.

The purpose of this section is to keep vendors from selling unpopular items. Requiring a list of the products before the bid opening can prevent a confrontation with the high bidder when its bid is discarded due to unacceptable products. This provision gives all bidders a chance to obtain product costs for quality items and submit bids on an equal basis. This contract requires that the products must be in the top 25 candies listed in the *National Candy Buyers Brands Survey*. The last sentence includes the current three top selling products on campus (other schools may want to specify more or less than three candies).

32.   Quality disposables and condiments will be supplied by the Vendor. All bidders must submit samples for written approval by the Director of Vending prior to bid opening.

If there is food involved in the bid that requires disposables, the school should approve, in writing, what each vendor is planning on using.

33. Products must be from fresh production. Day-old or outdated merchandise is not acceptable. Outdated products in the machines is the financial responsibility of the Vendor. The Vendor is responsible for removing from ABC property all empty boxes and containers used in supplying the machines.

This should be fairly obvious, but it does need to be stated. Put the vendors on notice that you want quality. It is the vendor's financial responsibility for outdated merchandise.

The last part of this condition prevents the vendor from stuffing boxes into the nearest trash can inside or outside the building.

34. Information stickers, supplied by the Vendor, must be attached to all machines. These stickers shall list repair and maintenance telephone numbers and hours. During normal business hours, customer complaints will be received by ABC employees. ABC employees in turn will telephone the Vendor at 9 A.M. and 2 P.M. to report problems. The after-hours telephone number must be the Vendor's local number or a toll-free number. Sticker information, layout, size, color and design must have ABC's written approval. Excessive customer complaints of any kind shall be cause of contract termination.

It should be stated in the contract who is going to supply the stickers. What is to be listed on the sticker can be set up after the contract award. Make sure the school has final approval, and it should be in writing.

The best method of keeping track of malfunctioning machines and product shortages is for the school to receive the telephone calls. If the calls are made directly to the vendor there is a chance that not all of them will be reported to the school. Use the school's telephone number during the day and the vendor's for emergencies after office hours.

It is conceivable that a vendor, operating from another town, is not in the local calling area. To avoid long distance charges, a local or toll-free number should be required.

The last sentence in condition 34 warns the vendors that the school considers customer complaints very important and that the continuation of the contract depends on customer satisfaction. If this is a major concern, you may want this sentence listed in a separate condition.

35. The Vendor awarded the contract must operate a local office and supply warehouse for the duration of this contract. No storage space is available on campus. The Vendor agrees that all offices and warehouses that service ABC shall be subject to inspection by any person designated by ABC at any reasonable times.

A local warehouse may or may not be important to the school. If there are many machines and the campus is not located in a major metropolitan area it could be important.

The school should have the right to inspect the vendor's facilities.

36. The Vendor receiving this contract must be able to show, through experience, the ability to handle an account of this size. Attach a list of three accounts currently being serviced and a contact person at each operation for reference. A financial report will be required of the high bidder.

A school with a number of machines may want to consider this condition. It states that each bidder must have the experience and financial ability to do the job properly. A number of companies are privately owned and are not interested in everyone knowing their finances. Therefore this condition asks for a financial statement only from the winning bidder.

37. During the life of this contract, ABC may want to lease equipment from the Vendor. Attach a letter indicating your charges (lease rate per machine, service call charges per hour and any other charges your firm would levy) for the following equipment:
1. Beverage, cold (standard 12-oz can with 6 selections, capacity 288 cans)
2. Beverage, hot (standard machine containing 5 selections: coffee, decaffeinated coffee, soup, hot chocolate, and tea)
3. Food, cold (standard machine containing a minimum of 8 selections)
4. Candy–chips (glass-front spiral, 40 selections)
5. Ice cream (standard machine with 3 selections)
6. Microwave oven (standard commercial grade, with pushbutton settings)
7. Milk–juice (standard machine containing a minimum of 6 selections)

Include type, manufacturer, model number and illustration for each machine.

Remember this is a 5-year contract and in the future a cafeteria or snack shop operation may be converted to vending for the summer or on a permanent basis. This will give the school the option of leasing equipment.

38.   This agreement constitutes the entire agreement between the parties with respect to the matters covered herein and there are no oral understandings or agreements with respect thereto. No variation or modification of this agreement and no waiver of its provisions shall be valid unless it is in writing and signed by the duly authorized officers of the Vendor and ABC. If agreeable to both Vendor and ABC, this contract may be extended.

Do not get caught just after the bid opening with the second highest bidder saying "Don't you remember our conversation? I told you my company would give the school a $10,000 scholarship each year. With that figured into the bid my company won." Be prepared in advance to avoid misunderstandings. *All agreements have to be in writing and approved by both parties.*

The last sentence in condition 38 may be set by school policy. Some schools do not allow any contract extensions; others allow 1-year extensions, and some extensions up to a maximum of one-half of the duration of the contract.

In compliance with and subject to all 38 conditions thereof, the undersigned offers and agrees to accept full responsibility for the complete operation and maintenance of all vending machines listed above. The undersigned agrees to remit to ABC the following percentages of the gross sales of this operation:

Beverage, cold	_____ %
Beverage, hot	_____ %
Candy–chips	_____ %
Cigarettes	_____ %
Food, cold	_____ %
Food, hot	_____ %
Ice cream	_____ %
Milk–juice	_____ %
Pastry	_____ %

Date _____

_____
Firm name

_____
Street

_____
City   State   Zip

_____
By (print name)

_____
By (signature)

_____
Title

ABC FOOD VENDING BID

March 6, 1986

The food vending contract will be awarded to the Vendor who meets all 38 requirements under General Conditions and offers the largest "Grand Total Commission" to ABC.

Listed below are the anticipated sales for the first year (12 months), July 1, 1986, through June 30, 1991, of this five (5) year contract.

Machines required*	Product	Anticipated gross sales ($)	Commission to ABC Percentage of gross (%)	($)
20	Beverage, cold	80,000		
8	Beverage, hot	12,000		
20	Candy–chips	70,000		
12	Cigarettes	28,000		
5	Food, cold	10,000		
2	Food, hot canned	4,000		
8	Milk–juice	10,000		
8	Ice cream	10,000		
5	Pastry	20,000		
2	Condiment stands	0		
5	Bill changer	0		
5	Microwave oven	0		
100 *See General Condition no. 20		$244,000		

Grand Total Commission $

Date _____

Firm name _____

Street _____

City _____ State _____ Zip _____

By: (print name) _____

By: (signature) _____

Title _____

FIG. 8.1. The calculation page of a sample vending contract to be filled out by each bidder. The Grand Total Commission section determines the high bidder.

ABC FOOD VENDING BID

March 6, 1986

The food vending contract will be awarded to the Vendor who meets all 38 requirements under General Conditions and offers the largest "Grand Total Commission" to ABC.

Listed below are the anticipated sales for the first year (12 months), July 1, 1986, through June 30, 1991, of this five (5) year contract.

Machines required*	Product	Anticipated gross sales ($)	Commission to ABC Percentage of gross (%)	Commission to ABC ($)
20	Beverage, cold	80,000	8	6,400
8	Beverage, hot	12,000	8	960
20	Candy–chips	70,000	8	5,600
12	Cigarettes	28,000	8	2,240
5	Food, cold	10,000	8	800
2	Food, hot canned	4,000	8	320
8	Milk–juice	10,000	8	800
8	Ice cream	10,000	8	800
5	Pastry	20,000	8	1,600
2	Condiment stands	0		
5	Bill changer	0		
5	Microwave oven	0		
100 *See General Condition no. 20		$244,000		

Grand Total Commission | $19,520

Date ___ March 1, 1986 ___

C. Gagliano Co.
Firm name

W. 187 Holmes Avenue
Street

Anywhere   U.S.A.
City   State   Zip

C. Gagliano
By: (print name)

C. Gagliano
By: (signature)

Sales Manager
Title

FIG. 8.2. Bid completed giving commissions to the school in terms of dollars and percentages.

ABC FOOD VENDING BID

March 6, 1986

The food vending contract will be awarded to the Vendor who meets all 38 requirements under General Conditions and offers the largest "Grand Total Commission" to ABC.

Listed below are the anticipated sales for the first year (12 months), July 1, 1986, through June 30, 1991, of this five (5) year contract.

Machines required*	Product	Anticipated gross sales ($)	Commission to ABC Percentage of gross (%)	Commission to ABC ($)
20	Beverage, cold	80,000	10	8,000
8	Beverage, hot	12,000	5	600
20	Candy–chips	70,000	12	8,400
12	Cigarettes	28,000	10	2,800
5	Food, cold	10,000	0	0
2	Food, hot canned	4,000	0	0
8	Milk–juice	10,000	5	500
8	Ice cream	10,000	5	500
5	Pastry	20,000	5	1,000
2	Condiment stands	0		
5	Bill changer	0		
5	Microwave oven	0		
100 *See General Condition no. 20		244,000		

Grand Total Commission | $21,800

Date _____ February 25, 1986

F. Economist Inc.
Firm name

150 Round Jackson Drive
Street

Anywhere _____ U.S.A. _____
City _____ State _____ Zip

F. Economist
By: (print name)

F. Economist
By: (signature)

President
Title

FIG. 8.3. Another completed bid by a vendor including commissions in dollars and percentages.

Now it is time for the bidders to respond to your request for service. What percentage commissions are the companies willing to give the school?

One of the blanks for the bidding company to fill in is "By: (print name)." Most of the time it is very hard, if not impossible, to read an executive's signature. It is most embarrassing to mispronounce or misspell a person's name. By requiring both the signature and printed name it will help in later dealings with the company.

In order to help the bidders calculate their costs and profits, they need to know what they can expect in sales. The information can be from last year's sales or an educated guess by the director of vending on anticipated sales for the first year of the new contract.

Figure 8.1 is part of the contract and is used to calculate whose bid is the highest. Whoever offers the highest Grand Total Commission and meets all 38 conditions will receive the contract award.

Figures 8.2 and 8.3 are examples of what two different companies might submit as bids.

In these samples, Economist Inc. would receive the contract as it has offered $2,280 more than Gagliano Company.

It is common for companies not to offer commissions on certain foods, such as sandwiches, pastries and fresh fruit. Due to its perishability and low profit margin there is not a lot of money to be made from these items unless there is a steady clientele and large volume.

Most customers use food vending machines on days when the weather is bad. When it rains or snows, or is very cold people do not want to go outside. On nice days machines are used less and food spoilage is greater. This is costly to the vendor.

Food machines can be profitable in locations that replace a cafeteria or snack shop. Here volume is high enough to prevent spoilage.

VENDING GOALS

A number of people do not like vending machines. Complaints are that they are impersonal and they malfunction. They are big, clumsy looking and create the potential for a messy area. On the other hand, they offer a service to people.

Most schools use some type of vending machines. The following is a list of goals to consider for the vending operations in the school:

1. Provide products and services in as many locations as necessary and practicable.
2. Charge fair prices for products or services offered.
3. Refill machines as often as needed to keep items fresh with no outages prior to scheduled refills.
4. Keep machines in a clean, operable working condition.
5. Produce optimum commissions for the school.

REFERENCES

MEHA. 1983. Michigan's Food Service Sanitation Regulations. Michigan Environmental Health Association, Lansing, MI.

NACUBO. 1982. Contracting for Services. National Association of College and University Business Offices, Washington, DC.

9 National Association of College and University Food Services

A number of national associations have college and university foodservices as part of their organization. The Association of College and University Housing Officers—International, the National Association of College Auxiliary Services, and the National Restaurant Association are three of these. One association comprised of only foodservice people, dedicated to the advancement of better foodservice for college students, is the National Association of College and University Food Services (NACUFS).

NACUFS is both a national and regional organization with four of the regions having international members (Fig. 9.1) and currently more than 500 schools are represented in the organization.

The national organization elects from its membership the following officers: president, president-elect, publications officer and treasurer.

Since these executive officers have a 1-year term, an administrative secretary has been appointed and a permanent office is maintained on the campus of Michigan State University. The secretary's address is Administrative Secretary, 7 Olds Hall, Michigan State University, East Lansing, MI 48824.

National Association
of College and University Food Services
OUR NINE REGIONS

Alaska
Australia
Canada
Caribbean
Hawaii
Hong Kong
Puerto Rico
Virgin Islands

REGION I   Connecticut, Maine, Massachusetts, New Hampshire, New York,
              Provinces of Ontario and Quebec, Rhode Island, Vermont.
REGION II   Delaware, District of Columbia, Maryland, New Jersey, Pennsylvania,
              Virginia, West Virginia.
REGION III   Alabama, Florida, Georgia, Kentucky, Mississippi, North Carolina, Puerto
              Rico, South Carolina, Tennessee, Virgin Islands.
REGION IV   Indiana, Illinois, Michigan, Ohio, Wisconsin.
REGION V   Minnesota, North Dakota, Province of Manitoba, South Dakota.
REGION VI   Missouri, Iowa, Nebraska, and Kansas.
REGION VII   Arkansas Louisiana, New Mexico, Oklahoma, Texas.
REGION VIII   Colorado, Idaho, Montana, Province of Alberta, Utah, Wyoming.
REGION IX   Alaska, Arizona, Australia, California, Hawaii, Hong Kong, Nevada, Oregon
              Province of British Columbia, Washington.

FIG. 9.1.   Map showing the nine regions in NACUFS.

CONSTITUTION

Membership in the organization is outlined in the constitution:

Our constitution states that membership shall be by school, college or university operating its own food service program. Institutions which have commercial caterers managing the food service organization may be members of NACUFS but only salaried staff of the institution may be active in association affairs and be allowed to vote.

Their association ideals are

Purpose

The purposes of NACUFS shall be to advance the highest standards of food service on school, college and university campuses; to provide a medium through which its members may jointly advance and promote their common interest, goals and objectives; to provide information and

TABLE 9.1. Standing Committees—NACUFS

Name	Goal
National Conference	To provide for the planning and implementation of the National Conference
National Industry Advisory Council	To provide a close working relationship and communications between the membership and industry
Professional Standards	To promote high standards of operations and professionalism within NACUFS
Public Affairs	To make the membership aware of current events that affect the food industry
Public Relations	To interpret the NACUFS purposes and activities to all segments of the Food Service Industry and its related publics
Audit	To monitor effectiveness of the association's management of the financial and accounting functions of its use of human and physical resources
Long Range Planning	To assess the long range program needs of the organization including financial concerns and make recommendations for appropriate action to the executive board
Education–Training	To assist, regionally and nationally, in the development and implementation of training programs, to collect and publish information about available training programs and resources and to develop and present a pre-conference seminar in coordination with the national conference chairman
Food and Nutrition Awareness	To provide membership with practical programs and methods for continually conveying food and nutrition information and awareness to the people we serve
Membership	To provide for the continued growth of NACUFS by making material available to prospective members and coordinating Regional and Central Office membership activities

TABLE 9.2. Excerpts from *NACUFS Professional Standards Manual*

Performance standards	Criteria
1. *Costs, Controls and Accountability—Annual Budget[a]*	
Projections of changes in expenses shall be established prior to fiscal year.	Projections of food and supplies expenses are made using current market reports, supplies information, and price histories.
	Labor contract obligations, future negotiations, and federal legislation are studied to project labor cost increases.
	Input from physical plant and utility companies are used to project energy cost increases.
	Records are kept of progression of costs for prior periods.
	Proposed equipment replacement and renovation expenses and major repairs expenses are documented.
Projected income shall be established for next fiscal year.	Enrollments and number of returning students, based on past histories, are projected.
2. *Satisfaction—Clientele[b]*	
The foodservice department shall have policies and procedures on evaluation of services.	Surveys are conducted periodically to determine satisfaction, and should include the following information:
	a. Timeliness of service hours
	b. Quality of the food and beverage
	c. Quantity and variety of food and beverage
3. *Systems for Quality Assurance—Menu[c]*	
Menu policies shall be established.	Daily minimum menu pattern policies are written.
	Guidelines on menu item frequency are written.
	Quality standards for menu items are established.
Menus shall be developed systematically.	An established procedure is identified and followed in developing menus.

assistance to membership by means of conferences, programs, publications, discussions and research; to advance the cause of good nutrition and to promote adventurous and desirable eating habits among students; work cooperatively with Professional Associations in the fields of Higher Education and the Food Service Industry towards the attainment of mutually compatible objectives.

NACUFS prints a number of publications through the year. These are listed in the Appendix.

MEETINGS AND COMMITTEES

Each region has a yearly meeting. There is a large national conference once a year in July. Meetings are rotated and hosted by a different school each year. This allows members to visit different schools and those with a small travel budget an opportunity to attend on a periodic basis.

TABLE 9.2.   *(Continued)*

Performance standards	Criteria

4. *Sanitation and Safety—Personal Sanitation[d]*

Personal sanitation and safety standards shall be established.	Employees are instructed on personal sanitation and safety requirements. New employee orientation programs cover accepted personal sanitation and safety requirements. Continual on-the-job personal sanitation and safety programs are conducted regularly.

5. *Personnel Administration—Recruitment and Staffing[e]*

A uniform, comprehensive, and effective employment system shall be established.	Reasonable employment standards are determined for each position. Fair and equal opportunity for employment is accorded to all qualified individuals.

6. *Programs—Nutrition Education[f]*

The foodservice department shall have an effective nutrition education program.	An effective nutrition education program for students, customers, and staff is operational.
The nutrition education program shall be designed by a registered dietitian.	The program is monitored by a registered dietitian or professionally qualified nutritionist.

[a]*Objective:* To establish income and expense goals, meet financial responsibilities, and measure progress through use of a budget.
[b]*Objective:* To operate a foodservice department that satisfies the needs of students, faculty, staff and administrators.
[c]*Objective:* To provide a menu system that satisfies customers and meets the goals of the foodservice department.
[d]*Objective:* To promote a safe environment in foodservice operations through personal employee sanitation.
[e]*Objective:* To maintain an efficient and effective work force.
[f]*Objective:* To provide an effective nutrition education program for clientele and employees.

NACUFS has established a number of national committees to meet the organization's goals. Foodservice professionals from across the country are appointed by the president to chair the committees on a 2-year basis. The standing committees and the goals are listed in Table 9.1.

THE CALL FOR STANDARDS

One of the most energetic undertakings in the 1970s was the development of a professional standards manual. A committee was formed of 11 NACUFS members, making sure each region was represented. It took 2 years to develop and 1 year to test and rewrite the manual and procedures into its final form.

The big questions at the outset were as follows: (1) Should it be for individuals or for schools? The certification of an individual would be comparable to that for a doctor, lawyer, nurse or dietitian—a test or series of tests to determine the person's knowledge. Certification of a school would be more complex. Since both management and labor personnel come and go, the knowledge and quality of the operation can change. Once a certification is made, how long should it be valid? Who would certify the school? With over 500 members it would require a large team of knowledgeable people to test each school. This would be very expensive and a number of schools would probably not be able to afford certification.

Self-Inspection

The answers to those questions resulted in a 65-page manual published in 1982 entitled *NACUFS Professional Standards Manual*. NACUFS has made this available to members and nonmembers.

The manual is divided into six parts:

1. Costs, controls and accountability
2. Customer satisfaction
3. Systems for quality assurance
4. Sanitation and safety
5. Personnel administration
6. Programming

TABLE 9.3.   NACUFS Institutions Visited by a Professional Standards Team

Region	School
1	University of Rochester
2	Dickinson College
	Lebanon Valley College
	University of Maryland
	University of Pennsylvania[a]
	Virginia Polytechnic Institute & University
3	North Carolina State University[a]
4	Michigan State University[a]
	Ohio State University[a]
5	None
6	None
7	Oklahoma State University[a]
	North Texas State University[a]
	Sam Houston State University
	University of Arkansas[a]
8	University of Montana
9	University of the Pacific

[a]Institutions with NACUFS members who have been on a professional standards team visiting another school.

NACUFS PROFESSIONAL STANDARDS
WORKSHEET

SECTION: ____________

PAGE: ____________

DATE: ____________

STANDARD NUMBER	COMPLY	DEFICIENCY	NOT APPLICABLE	COMMENTS

DUPLICATION OF THE WORKSHEET PORTION ONLY OF THIS COPYRIGHTED MANUAL IS PERMITTED.

White copy: Unit Manager
Yellow copy: Evaluator
Pink copy: Director

FIG. 9.2. Worksheet used by teams of NACUFS professionals in assessing quality standards of a foodservice facility.

Table 9.2 shows samples of each area covered.

The six parts are divided into subgroups, listing the overall objectives of that section. Performance standards are stated for each section.

This is a self-study, self-inspection manual. There are in reality no right or wrong ways to meet the standards. School policies and procedures, along with state regulations, may influence how a standard is met or not met. A school in southern California may meet the criteria differently than one in Mississippi. Furthermore, since NACUFS is an international organization, a school in British Columbia may have a different way of meeting the standards.

The criteria are general, not specific. The manual does not state how the standards are to be met. Most can be read as a question—do you? Can a school answer "Yes, we do that. We do it thus and so."? The thus and so can be different from school to school.

As an example, the manual says "All menu displays are correct in pricing and spelling." It does not say what kind of menu boards you should have. The standards manual says you should have one and that the pricing and spelling should be correct. This forces you as a professional to look at your menu boards and check its accuracy. If it is correct—fine, but if you offer the excuse "we ran out of S letters, that's why some words are misspelled," that is not very professional. It does not matter that the students can guess what the menu items are.

Peer Inspection

The standards manual can be used for self-inspection, or your school can request a team of peers from member institutions to compare your operation to the standards established in the manual.

During NACUFS' first year of inspections by peers, the team visited 15 schools (Table 9.3). Over 30 different NACUFS members in teams of from two to seven people spent 4 days at each campus.

As team members made personal observations and interviewed staff and students they recorded their findings on a three-copy worksheet (Fig. 9.2).

At the end of the visitation the schools were given the reports. Outside of the inspection team and the host school, the report is not shared with anyone else.

The manual can be used for several inspections. Each year it is hoped that the professionals in NACUFS will review their operation against the performance standards and criteria outlined in the manual.

REFERENCES

NACUFS. Directory Update (current year). National Association of College and University Food Services. East Lansing, MI.

NACUFS. Professional Standards Manual, 1982. National Association of College and University Food Services. East Lansing, MI.

RICHIE, D. H. 1983. The First Twenty-Five Years, NACUFS 1958 to 1983. National Association of College and University Food Services, East Lansing, MI.

CAS. Memorandum dated December 27, 1983. Council for the Advancement of Standards for Student Services/Development Programs, Washington, DC.

Appendix

Selected Trade Publications and Associations

HOW TO SELECT

Where a person is in the industry will determine which publications should be subscribed to. Most people running a food operation will read general publications, association newsletters and local newspapers. Those in research, sales and manufacturing will subscribe to more technical publications affecting their area of the industry. A school that has a central bake shop should subscribe to some baking journals and, if it has a meat cutting operation, the *National Provisioner Magazine*.

The more specialized the job the more specialized the reading should be. Another criterion to use is what needs to be known to keep abreast of the markets and trends in the field?

If you have nothing to do with vending, why bother with *Vending Times* or *Automatic Merchandizer?* On the other hand, if the school is planning to convert or augment its operation with vending machines, it should request a subscription.

General publications such as *Institutions* and *Nation's Restaurant News* cover so many areas of interest that they usually do not give much space to warnings of what the future may be.

Take a hypothetical situation and see how it may be covered in various publications:

A heat wave is spreading through the South. The poultry industry is concerned that it could cause a high mortality rate in chickens. This would mean some unavailability of certain sized birds for processing and also increased prices in all poultry products.

1.   On one hand, *Broiler Industry* magazine will probably spend a good deal of space on the subject, with a history of what took place the last time it happened, and some projections of what they think may happen. The heat wave is big news for this publication.

2.   On the other hand, the general foodservice magazine editors will have to consider the heat wave story against all of their other areas of interest. Probably their thought processes will be something like this: "There is a heat wave and it *might* affect the poultry industry. Let's see what happens, and next month, if there is going to be a shortage, we can do an article. If, just before deadline, it still looks like it might be a major problem, we can print a small paragraph or two alerting our readers." If the general publication spent its time and space doing large "what-if" articles, they would not be able to print anything else. There is no way that they can spend the research time and devote the space to "maybe" situations that a specialty magazine can.

The heat wave will generate interest on the part of the poultry magazine to contact manufacturers in the air-conditioning and air-circulating industry. At the same time, manufacturers of that kind of equipment will be getting in touch with magazines for advertising space. Again, the heat wave is big news for the poultry magazine, but of only future interest to the general foodservice publication.

If a manager is responsible for an operation that has chicken on its menu only once in a while, then the general publication gives enough information. The current edition stating that there is a potential problem, with the follow-up next month if it actually happens, is probably sufficient.

On the other hand, if the school runs a fast food operation on campus that specializes in chicken that accounts for 75% of its sales, the manager should know as much about the chicken industry as possible. This appendix lists some publications that managers should consider reading to keep abreast of markets and trends.

FOODSERVICE TRADE PUBLICATIONS

Periodicals are like computer printouts; there are so many, with so much information that you could spend all your time reading them.

Companies are very receptive to requests from managers inquiring about their publications. Remember they are in the business of making a profit, and one way of doing that is to increase their circulation.

Technical Publications

Food Processing (monthly). Putman Publishing Company, 301 East Erie Street, Chicago, IL 60611.

Processed Prepared Foods (monthly). 5725 East River Road, Chicago, IL 60631.

Both publications are designed for research and development departments at food manufacturing companies.

General Publications

Cooking for Profit (monthly). P.O. Box 267, Fond du Lac, WI 54935. A general magazine on the food industry with high emphasis on food preparation.

Consumers Reports (monthly). P.O. Box 1919, Marion, OH 43306. This magazine compares and rates products and equipment for the retail consumer. A number of items are relative to the institutional foodservice business.

Food Management (monthly). 1 East First Street, Duluth, MN 55802. In addition to food, articles are about general management problems and outlooks.

Foodservice Product News (monthly). 104 Fifth Avenue, New York, NY 10011. Ads, ads, ads—food, equipment and supplies.

Independent Restaurants (monthly). 2132 Fordem Avenue, Madison, WI 53704. Formerly *Food Service Marketing*. Directed toward the independent operators and their problems of decor, menu, advertising and management.

Nation's Restaurant News (25 issues/year). Subscription Department, 99 Park Avenue, New York, NY 10157. Primarily deals with company facts, figures, management moves and announcements.

Restaurant Business (9 issues/year). 633 Third Avenue, New York, NY 10017. A magazine covering the business aspect of the restaurant field.

Restaurant & Institutions (bi-monthly). Cahners Publishing Co., 270 St. Paul Street, Denver, CO 80206. A general publication aimed at all phases of the foodservice industry.

Western Food Service (monthly). Western Foods, 342 Madison Avenue, New York, NY 10173. A general foodservice magazine featuring food operations in the western part of the United States.

Specific Segments of the Industry

Airconditioning & Refrigeration Business (monthly). 614 Superior Avenue West, Cleveland, OH 44113. This magazine, for the airconditioning and refrigeration business, is probably more suited for the engineers in the physical plant department.

American Automatic Merchandise (monthly). 1 East First Street, Duluth, MN 55802. All about vending machines, products, service and maintenance.

Baking Industry (monthly). Putman Publishing Co., 301 East Erie Street, Chicago, IL 60611. This is for the person with the responsibility for a central baking operation.

Beverage Industry (monthly). Circulation Department, 1 East First Street, Duluth, MN 55802. Soft drink, beer and wine information for the beverage industry; particularly helpful for those in vending.

Broiler Industry (monthly). Circulation Department, Watt Publishing Co., Mount Morris, IL 61054. Aimed at the producer, processor and wholesaler of chickens, this magazine gives current and future prices.

Buildings (monthly). Stamats Communications Inc., 427 Sixth Avenue Southeast, Cedar Rapids, IA 52406. A publication for contractors and builders. Renovations and building maintenance are key topic areas.

Business Computer Systems (monthly). P.O. Box 17452, Denver, CO 80217. This is only one of many computer magazines on the market.

Cooking for Profit (monthly). P.O. Box 267, Fond du Lac, WI 54935. A general magazine on the food industry with high emphasis on food preparation.

Cleaning Management (monthly). 17911-C Sky Park Boulevard, Irvine, CA 92714. All you ever wanted to know about being a custodian. Products, equipment, methods and procedures.

Dealer Food Service Equipment (monthly). 270 St. Paul Street, Denver, CO 80206. This is a publication about foodservice equipment for the wholesaler. It is interesting to read since it contains articles on how to sell to the foodservice operator.

Distribution (monthly). Chilton Way, Radnor, PA 19089. A warehousing publication, not designed for a storeroom in a cafeteria or restaurant, but for a central warehouse or wholesale operation.

Engineer's Digest (monthly). Walker-Davis Publication, Inc., 2500 Office Center, Willow Grove, PA 19090. If you have a physical plant department with engineers and there is no need to use outside contractors, this publication will not be very useful.

Foodservice Equipment Specialist (monthly). Circulation Office, 270 St. Paul Street, Denver, CO 80206. A magazine for the wholesale equipment dealer.

Food Institute Report (weekly). The American Institute of Food Distributors, Inc., 28-12 Broadway, Fair Lawn, NJ 07410. At one time this was three different reports—*Food Markets, Washington Food Report* and *Food Distribution*. The Food Markets section reports availability and current wholesale costs of most food items; the Washington section covers legislation, and the Food Distribution section reports on everything from population trends to food spending habits and consumption patterns.

Handling & Shipping Management (monthly). Circulation Department, P.O. Box 95759, Cleveland, OH 44101. Designed for shipping and warehousing operations.

Hotels & Restaurant International (bi-monthly). Circulation Records, Cahners Publishing Co., 270 St. Paul Street, Denver, CO 80206. Everything about hotels here and abroad; building, renovating, housekeeping and foodservice. The foodservice areas deal with gourmet foods.

Kiplinger Agricultural Letter (weekly). The Kiplinger Washington Editors, 1729 H Street Northwest, Washington, DC 20006. Written for farmers, but read by purchasing agents and business people, this publication gives market and crop productions, future trends and predictions on government regulations.

Material Handling Engineering (monthly). P.O. Box 95759, Cleveland, OH 44101. Warehouse equipment, supplies and procedures.

Michigan Farmer (21 issues/year). The Harvest Publishing Co., P.O. Box 6296, Duluth, MN 55806. This is a regional publication for the farmer. Many states have their own publications. If your school is a state-supported institution you should be aware of what is grown and processed in the state and what is taking place in the agriculture industry.

Modern Office Technology (monthly). P.O. Box 91368, Cleveland, OH 44101. All you ever wanted to know about office equipment, layout, design, procedures and forms.

National Provisioner (weekly). 15 West Huron Street, Chicago, IL 60610. A meat processing publication. A large number of photographs and text on specific meat packers and processors.

Plant Energy Management (monthly). Walker-Davis Publications, Inc., P.O. Box 482, 2500 Office Center, Willow Grove, PA 19090. This publication is designed for engineers.

Quick Frozen Foods (monthly). 1 East First Street, Duluth, MN 55802. A general frozen foods publication.

Restaurant Design (quarterly). Restaurant Business, Inc., 633 Third Avenue, New York, NY 10017. Deals with design and furnishings.

Seafood Business Report (quarterly). 21 Elm Street, Camden, ME 04843. Covers the three major areas: retail, foodservice and processing.

Seafood Leader (five issues/year). 1115 Northwest 46th Street, Seattle, WA 98107. Reports on technology, availability and marketing for the whole industry—fisherman, processor, broker, wholesaler, foodservice and grocer—are presented in this publication.

Vending Times (monthly). 211 East 43rd Street, New York, NY 10017. A newspaper of vending, feeding and recreational services.

Market Reports

Meat Price Report (weekly). National Provisioner, Inc., 15 West Huron Street, Chicago, IL 60610.

National Provisional Daily (daily). National Provisioner, Inc., 15 West Huron Street, Chicago, IL 60610. National Provisioner Inc. publishes two price lists. One, the *Meat Price Report,* because of its color is commonly called the *Green Sheet.* It lists the prices paid by restaurants for cuts of beef, pork, lamb and veal. Prices are listed for three grades and usually have a $0.04–$0.05 spread for each item. It is printed every Saturday. The *National Provisional Daily* or the *Yellow Sheet,* lists the daily prices paid by packers for primals and sub-primals of beef, pork, lamb and veal. Generally, the *Green Sheet* will be more useful to the foodservice operator as it is a guide to current meat prices.

Urner Barry's Price-Current (weekly). 182 Queens Boulevard, P.O. Box 312, Bayville, NJ 08721. Market quotations on cheese, butter, eggs, chickens, ducks, turkeys and game birds. Designed for the processor and wholesaler.

USDA Crop Reporting Board Publications. Room 5829, South Building USDA, Washington, DC 20250. Listed are the reports available:

Publication title	Month issued	Publication title	Month issued
Cherries—June 15	June	Hop Stocks—Sept. 1	September
Cherry Utilization	October	Meat Animals: Product, Disposition & Income	April
Citrus Fruits	September		
Commercial Fertilizer	November	Minn. Wis. Milk Price Series	June
Cranberries	August	Mushrooms	August
Crop Value	January	Peanut Stocks & Processing—Jan. 31	March
Farm Labor	August	Peanut Stocks & Processing—July 31	September
Farm Production Expenditures Summary	June	Turkey Hatchery	Monthly
		Sheep & Goats	January
Hop Stocks—Mar. 1	March		

USDA Crop Reporting Board Reports. Superintendent of Documents, U.S. Government Printing Office, Washington, DC 20402. The publications available are

Agricultural Price (12 issues)
Agricultural Price Summaries (2 issues)
Cattle (14 issues)
Celery (12 issues)
Cold Storage (13 issues)
Crop Production (16 issues)

Dairy Products (13 issues)
Egg Products (12 issues)
Egg, Chickens & Turkey (16 issues)
Grain Stocks (5 issues)
    Grain Stocks (4)
    Soybean Stocks (1)

Hogs and Pigs (4 issues)
Livestock Slaughter (13 issues)
Milk Production (13 issues)
Non-Citrus Fruits (2 issues)
Potatoes and Sweetpotatoes (7 issues)
   Potato Stocks (6)
   Potatoes and Sweetpotatoes (1)

Poultry Slaughter (12 issues)
Rice Stocks (4 issues)
Vegetables (13 issues)

Newspapers

The Packer (weekly). Circulation Department, P. O. Box 400, Prairie View, IL 60069. This publication deals with fresh fruits and vegetables. Designed for the wholesaler but useful to a foodservice operator. Current growing conditions, forecasts, how to handle products.

Wall Street Journal (daily). 1100 Brim Road, Bowling Green, OH 43402. A general financial newspaper, with a daily commodities section dealing with the future market. Also lists the daily market prices for the major crops.

Your local newspaper. Major events, frosts, bumper crops, etc., are reported as they occur. Some papers have a daily or weekly food column.

ASSOCIATIONS WITH RELEVANT PUBLICATIONS

Association of College & University Housing. Officers-International (ACUHO) (5 issues/year). The officers change each year and therefore the addresses also change. Check with the colleges in your area for the current mailing address.

National Association of College, Auxiliary Services (NACAS) (6 issues/year). P.O. Box 870, Staunton, VA 24401. Shares ideas and information among members.

National Association of College and University Food Services (NACUFS) (6 issues/year). Administrative Secretary, NACUFS, 7 Olds Hall, East Lansing, MI 48824. NACUFS prints a number of publications throughout the year:

   1. *A Newsletter–Digest* (4 issues/year). Includes information for the membership of national interest, articles of professional interest, regional news, conference news and industry news.

   2. *Facts and Findings* (monthly). This is a sharing of thoughts, ideas, accomplishments and tidbits of information on timely material. Each regional president, NACUFS president, NACUFS president-elect and the administrative secretary serve as editors on a rotating basis.

3. *Regional Newsletters* are printed according to regional guidelines and schedules.

4. *The Journal of the National Association of College and University Food Services* (annually). Articles of a professional nature are solicited from members, faculty-staff members not related to foodservice on member campuses, foodservice trade journal editors and associates.

Specialized publications, such as the standards and cash operations manuals and quantity recipe cookbooks, are printed and distributed to members.

National Restaurant Association (NRA) (monthly). NRA Headquarters, 311 First Street Northwest, Washington, DC 20001. This journal encompasses all types of foodservice operations: fast food, table cloth, hospitals, schools and cafeterias.

State Restaurant Association. Most states have their own restaurant associations. Contact restaurants in your area for details.

Publications of other associations (councils, commissions, institutes, boards and societies) designed by, for and about their particular subjects can be helpful. Their products are used by our industry and therefore the results of their ideas, testing and marketing should be of interest. Examples of large organizations include American Meat Institute, National Pork Producers Council, National Livestock and Meat Board, and the American Dairy Association. Examples of lesser known organizations would be American Beefalo Association, American Buffalo Association, American Dairy Goat Association, American Rabbit Breeders Association and the Sweet Potato Council of the United States.

Name the food and there are three to ten groups waiting to help. The school library reference section can help you locate names and addresses in the area where you have questions.

Index